Success with Inclusion

Today's classroom welcomes diversity, where many levels, speeds and styles of learning coexist. *Success with Inclusion* provides over 1000 specific strategies to help in identified areas of difficulty or advanced development. Using this book teachers will be able to:

- identify and record quickly and easily their pupils' individual learning patterns using the observation charts provided;
- structure a well-planned inclusive environment;
- implement creative and thoughtful learning interventions;
- create an atmosphere of flexibility and compassion.

Author and experienced teacher Glynis Hannell gets down to the nitty-gritty with chapters full of practical and creative ideas that will help accommodate not only pupils with difficulties but also those who are more advanced. Learning strategies here will help you to:

- be an effective inclusive teacher;
- address a variety of reading difficulties;
- support pupils' writing skills;
- make maths comprehensible, fun and relevant;
- enhance pupils' concentration;
- encourage habits of organisation;
- foster teamwork between yourself, colleagues, parents and pupils.

The 42 photocopiable worksheets, checklists, charts, games and planners are provided in an appendix to give teachers a head start. Also included are observation charts, literacy and maths resources, as well as support material for teachers, pupils and parents.

Glynis Hannell was formerly a psychologist in private practice and a lecturer in educational psychology at the University of South Australia.

Success with Inclusion

1001 teaching strategies and activities
that really work

Glynis Hannell

Routledge
Taylor & Francis Group

LONDON AND NEW YORK

First published 2007 by Peynal Publications in the USA

This edition published in the UK and Canada 2008
by Routledge
2 Park Square, Milton Park, Abingdon, Oxon OX14 4RN

Routledge is an imprint of the Taylor & Francis Group, an informa business

© 2007, 2008 Glynis Hannell

Typeset in Galliard by
HWA Text and Data Management, Tunbridge Wells
Printed and bound in Great Britain by
TJ International Ltd, Padstow, Cornwall

British Library Cataloguing in Publication Data
A catalogue record for this book is available from the British Library

Library of Congress Cataloging-in-Publication Data
Hannell, Glynis.
Success with inclusion : 1001 teaching strategies and activities that really
work / Glynis Hannell.
    p. cm.
Includes bibliographical references and index.
  1. Inclusive education—United States. 2. Activity programs in
education—United States. 3. Children with disabilities—Education—
United States. I. Title. II. Title: 1001 teaching strategies and activities
that really work. III. Title: One thousand and one teaching strategies
and activities that really work.
LC1201.H36 2007
371.9'0460973—dc22   2007013200

ISBN10: 0–415–44534–5
ISBN13: 978–0–415–44534–4

Contents

Introduction

Has there ever been a pupil who did not have 'learning differences'? Probably not! Every single human being on the face of the earth is unique. That is something we take for granted. Out of all the billions of people in the world, no one has exactly your face, your way of walking or your way of learning.

As teachers, we know that the amazing diversity and variety of the human race is reflected in every group we teach. We wouldn't believe it if all our pupils looked and behaved the same and had the same way of learning! Working effectively with diversity, variety and differences is at the very foundation of what good teachers do best.

Some of the qualities attributed to a good teacher are that he or she:

- develops ways to reach all pupils
- never forgets what it is like to be a learner – vulnerable, anxious or dependent
- is able to change teaching techniques to meet various pupils' needs
- has a big HEART
- sets the foundation – makes a difference
- enables all the pupils in the class to live better lives

In the following chapters, you will find a wealth of information on *intervention* and *inclusive education* (or simply referred to as *inclusion*) as well as numerous specific strategies for implementing these approaches to teaching.

Intervention involves explicit teaching and targeted instruction. Intervention is when teachers teach in the ways that the pupils learn.

Inclusive education (or inclusion) involves the use of a range of strategies to ensure that pupils with learning differences are full members of the classroom and school community. Inclusive education is how teachers can make a difference and enable all pupils to live better lives. It is not limited to pupils with special needs but includes all pupils with diverse needs.

Are intervention and inclusion extra things that teachers do on top of their regular work? No! Intervention and inclusion are what good teachers do all the time! Therefore, this book is a practical resource for all educators who want to be *good teachers* and *make a difference* to *all* the pupils they teach.

Chapter 1

Effective teaching

Introduction

This chapter will explain some of the basic foundations of effective teaching. How does the brain actually learn? That, in itself, is a miracle. To be effective as teachers, we need to understand the gradual, biological process we call learning, because as teachers, we actually make a difference – a real, physical difference – to the way our pupils' brains develop.

We also need to understand individual differences in learning capability and learning style. Then, we can adjust our teaching to the unique capacities of the individual pupils in our classes. Teachers who can do this are not only working hard, they are working smart!

Apart from inborn intelligence, every pupil has a range of personal qualities such as curiosity, persistence, self-confidence and so forth. The effective teacher can nurture these qualities and make a substantial difference in the quality of their pupils' learning.

Take a moment to reflect upon your own schooldays. Which teacher had the greatest positive impact upon you? In all probability, it was the teacher who built your confidence, encouraged your persistence and excited your curiosity. This chapter provides a range of ideas for developing these positive learning characteristics in all of your pupils.

The chapter ends with some thoughts on creating an inclusive classroom. *Being* included in a group and *feeling* included can be two, quite different situations. The effective teacher does not just do inclusive things. The effective teacher builds a classroom community where inclusion is part of the social fabric of the group of pupils and adults who work together.

The following Appendix forms are referenced in this chapter in the order given:

Appendix Form 24: 'Teacher checklist for successful learning'
Appendix Form 26: 'Teacher chart for planning an inclusive programme'
Appendix Form 23: 'Teacher checklist for mastery learning'
Appendix Form 30: 'Pupil guide to making changes'
Appendix Form 33: 'Pupil guide to setting goals'
Appendix Form 35: 'Pupil self-evaluation'
Appendix Form 39: 'Pupil notes: getting ready for a meeting'
Appendix Form 36: 'Pupil: what i think about school'
Appendix Form 37: 'Pupil reward cards'
Appendix Form 38: 'Pupil guide to "I can do"'.

The brain and learning

Teachers – part of the miracle

The human brain is a miracle. From the earliest days of life, the cells of the human brain are organising themselves into networks that communicate with each other, store and process information and learn new things. As teachers, we are part of this miracle. What we do in class will have a direct influence on how the pupils' brains develop. How does this happen?

The developing brain

The human brain has at least 100 billion neurons (brain cells). Each neuron has a cell body and a tree-like structure of branches called dendrites. The dendrites reach out and connect with each other at junctions called synapses.

The synapses are a very important part of the brain's information highway. Information is processed, stored and retrieved through the network of neurons and synapses. The more these networks are used, the more the connections build up, so things become easier and easier to do.

A child is equipped with many more neurons and synapses than they will ever need. The networks that are used grow stronger and more complex. Those that are unused may become lost. If teachers provide the right learning experiences, brain development is enhanced and accelerated.

Some brain systems, such as those for language and vision, have critical periods for development. Once the critical stage has passed, it is very difficult to fully develop the networks of cells needed for that particular function.

For example, babies with amblyopia, or 'lazy eye', are born with one eye weaker than the other. The good eye may become dominant, and information from the weaker eye may be ignored. If this happens, the synapses connecting the weaker eye to the brain will fail to develop, because these synapses are not being used. Permanently impaired vision may result. That is why doctors often patch the good eye. They are trying to force the pathways from the weaker eye to develop before the synapses are permanently lost. There is a window of opportunity in early childhood for this to happen. If it is not developed during this time period, often those particular synapses in the visual pathways are lost, and the sight cannot be restored.

However, within limits, some new synapses will form 'on demand' throughout life. As an adult, you may not have developed your 'piano playing' synapses, for example. But what happens if you take lessons and practice? Slowly and surely, you will find that your brain begins to build up a 'piano playing' network of neurons that was not there before. If you skip lessons and don't bother to practice, you will find that your synapses won't develop, no matter how much you want to be able to play!

Whether you are a concert pianist, a Grade I pupil or even a rat on a wheel, the principle is the same. Learning makes a physical difference to your brain.

Scientists set up an experiment with four groups of rats.

Group 1:   Exercise on a wheel for a set time each day
Group 2:   Unlimited access to an exercise wheel
Group 3:   No exercise
Group 4:   Obstacle course in which the rats had to learn challenging acrobatic
             moves.

When the rats' synapses were counted at the end of the four-week period, the outright winners were Group 4. All that learning on the obstacle course had built up new brain connections that had not been there before. Simply exercising without thinking had not made new connections.

Learning, then, is a gradual, accumulative biological process. Networks are activated and strengthened through experiences. The result is something we call learning. As teachers, we are in the front-line of managing this remarkable process. That's quite a challenge!
Following are some questions frequently asked by teachers.

Q.   If brains develop through experience and teaching, why can't I get all my pupils to the same level?

Brains are all unique, so your pupils will all have different starting points for learning. Some pupils are well equipped to learn new things quickly, others develop synapses more slowly. Some have good neural networks already established in, say, language, but less well developed networks in mathematics.

Q.   Can't the pupils just learn things (like times tables) by heart when they do not understand?

If they learn things by heart, they will develop a little mini-circuit of synapses. This might work quite well if all they have to do is recite the information. But the circuit probably will not connect into any other brain networks, so the memorised information will not be used in new situations.

Q.   Couldn't my pupils learn more quickly if they tried harder?

Of course effort is important to 'turn on' the brain activity that is needed. But remember that if the underlying synapses are not established, then structured, gradual work is needed to build up the necessary pathways. No amount of trying harder will produce a surge in brain networks without the necessary learning experiences.

Q.   I have a pupil who finds the class work too difficult. Surely she just needs to practice the same as everyone else.

Practice works really well when the connections at the synapses are just forming. Extra practice at this stage will strengthen the connections between brain cells. If the pupil does not have the early beginnings of the connections, then she will not have anything to build on. In this case, you will need to go back to find an earlier, simpler network that is already beginning to function. Once this is strengthened, then you will be able to move forward to new learning, step by step.

Q.   I have another pupil who learns everything quickly. She seldom makes mistakes. Surely she needs to practice just the same as everyone else.

When synapses are really well established, the brain networks function with high speed and accuracy. The pupils can perform tasks automatically, without the need for thinking or applying a great deal of effort. In this case, further routine practice is not needed and can be very frustrating to the pupil. The pupil needs to move on to activities that will begin to develop new connections and networks, building on the existing framework.

Q.   Once the networks of synapses have developed, will they stay forever?

Good strong networks of synapses are quite resilient. Some areas of learning are more permanent than others. For instance, we never forget how to ride a bike, even though we may easily forget our secondary school chemistry. There is usually some fading away over time, although often the network can be restored quite quickly, if it is reactivated. For example, you could probably relearn your chemistry much more quickly than the first time you tackled it, because some of the old connections are still there. Occasional practice can be helpful to make sure that earlier networks are still in good condition.

However, networks that are barely established and still in a fragile state will easily fall into disrepair if they are not exercised enough and given the chance to build up.

Q.   What about 'left brain' and 'right brain' learners?

While it is true that some functions are localised, the two hemispheres of the brain usually work in a closely integrated and highly complex way as a single unit. Indeed, even localisation can vary. For instance, most of us have our language centers in our left hemispheres, but there are quite frequent exceptions to this rule. About 10 percent of us have language in the right hemisphere. All of us have different patterns of interests and styles of thinking, and usually both sides of the brain are involved in any type of complex thinking.

Strategies for working with the developing brain

✱ Because some synapses are lost forever when they are not used, it is very important to identify developmental difficulties as early as you can. Always investigate concerns promptly, so intervention can start as soon as possible, if this proves necessary.

✱ Look for the level of difficulty where the pupil can *almost* complete the task unaided but needs a little help to succeed. Plan your teaching to strengthen existing connections and networks, and gradually build up more complex ones.

✱ Use prompting to help pupils use existing networks for thinking. Observe pupils as they work. Remind the pupils of the next steps, ask questions that will help them to think along the right track or provide clues so pupils begin to activate the networks that are needed for the task.

✱ Provide guided practice activities to help your pupils develop the brain systems they need to complete the learning tasks. As they experiment with a new task or skill, provide guidance so they see for themselves how to proceed through the steps to successful achievement. Going through the correct procedures helps to make brain connections.

✱ Watch for pupils who are developing incorrect habits, for example in handwriting, spelling or mathematics calculations. It is often very difficult to develop a new network when an existing one is already firmly established.

✱ Use questioning to activate the pupil's existing understanding. Ask more questions to help develop new connections: 'What happens to water left on a saucer in the sun? … Where does it go? … What do you think happens to the water in the ocean? … Where does it go?'

✱ Brains that are actively engaged learn. Structure your activities so that all pupils have to think and use their brains at the level that is appropriate to their development.

✱ Be cautious when using activities such as colouring or copying words as teaching tools. These activities will not necessarily contribute to brain development unless some mental activity is required.

✱ Improve the teaching value of colouring by stimulating thinking. For example, ask the pupils to colour in only the things that can grow or make all the metal red and all the plants green.

✱ Improve copying tasks with instructions such as, 'When you have copied it down, read it through and draw a line under all the description words,' or 'Copy the sentences, then highlight the most important words in each sentence'.

✱ Plan your teaching to provide all pupils with the appropriate level of input and support. Pupils who find learning difficult will need more structure and support with their tasks. For example, you might provide a framework of headings for an essay, or break the task up into small sections, so the work is manageable for the pupil.

✱ When pupils learn very quickly and easily, adjust your teaching so the pupils are working at their own 'boundaries of competence' and their brains are continuing to develop in new areas of learning.

✱ Provide a plan or diagram of how to work through a task, step-by-step. This road map of how to think things through will help the pupils to develop their own thinking and make real connections with their learning.

✱ Appropriate levels of practice are important to strengthen the brain circuits necessary for long-term learning. Pupils with special needs often need more practice than most other pupils to reach a reasonable level of competence.

✱ Continue teaching and reinforcing until the pupil has a strong grasp of new learning so you know that the underlying structures are well developed and are more likely to be resilient.

✱ If pupils forget new learning too quickly, this tells you that they have not had sufficient consolidation during the period of instruction and practice.

✱ Accept that pupils will not be able to bypass foundation learning. Learning is an accumulation process based on neurological development.

✳ Remember that pupils cannot suddenly produce brain structures that have not been built up by earlier experience, teaching or learning.

✳ The term *left-brain learner* or *right-brain learner* can confuse and worry pupils and parents. It is probably better to describe how the pupil learns, such as, 'This pupil works best when we use demonstrations and pictures to teach', or 'This pupil enjoys language'.

Individual learning differences

Innate learning capabilities

As mentioned in the previous section, learning depends on the gradual development of systems within the brain that can process information. Each individual has a unique pattern of mental development that is determined by innate capabilities interacting with the environment.

For the most part, the growth in mental ability follows a timetable that is reasonably predictable. For example, we can say that the norm is for children to begin using single words by the time they are about 12 to 18 months old. But we also know that wide variations are to be expected.

In school, some pupils seem to be fairly average at most things, others may have general learning difficulties, and some will be more advanced than the majority of their classmates. Some pupils will excel in some areas and be delayed in others. Such a mix of patterns is normal. It would be very unusual to have a class of pupils in which there was not a wide variation of abilities. Only in classes where the pupils have been selected according to their learning abilities would you expect some similarities – but even in this situation, there will never be complete uniformity.

Moving from concrete to abstract thinking

Infants begin life thinking only about the here and now – what they can see or touch and what is happening at that very moment. If a toy is moved out of view, it also seems to move out of mind, and the baby has no further interest in it. This type of thinking is called 'concrete thinking'.

Concrete thinking can continue throughout life. Even as adults, we want a diagram to show us how to put a table together, we try on a hat rather than just imagine what it will look like, we find it easier to understand a recipe than a chemical formula and we are more interested in a news item about our own neighbourhood than about a place on the other side of the world.

However as children mature, they begin to be able to think about things that are more remote and not necessarily based in their real and immediate world. They also begin to be able to think about 'what if' situations, ideas and values that may have little or no connection to real events or objects. This type of thinking is called 'abstract thinking', and it is a very important part of learning and life skills.

Teachers work with pupils to develop the pupils' capacity to move from the concrete to the abstract in gradual stages. For example, a pupil begins mathematics with concrete objects to count. Gradually, the teacher introduces tasks where thinking replaces physical action. Several years later, the pupil may be working with mathematics theories and calculations that are essentially mental and not concrete processes at all.

Every pupil will go through the same stages of development in exactly the same sequence. However, the speed at which individual pupils will achieve various stages of thinking will vary considerably.

Some pupils will move through the stages of development more slowly. For example, a 12-year-old may be using thinking skills usually more typical of an 8-year-old. Compared with most of their age group, this pupil will need to be taught using more concrete methods and will be less able to cope with teaching that requires abstract reasoning.

Concrete thinking also impacts socialisation. The pupil who is delayed in the development of abstract reasoning may find it hard to keep pace with the thinking and ideas of the peer group. The pupil may seem slow to catch on to the rules of a game or to understand a joke. This pupil may take things more literally, rely more heavily on their own experience and be less able to use 'what if' thinking in social situations.

Pupils who develop significantly more slowly may remain at a very concrete stage of thinking right through late adolescence and into adulthood.

In IQ tests, children are sometimes asked to say how pairs of items are the same. The concrete thinkers give answers such as, 'An apple and a banana are the same because they both have skin', or 'A dog and a cat are the same because they're both fluffy.' Their answers relate to physical qualities and personal experience.

The pupils who are abstract thinkers give answers such as, 'An apple and a banana are both nutritious fruit'. Sometimes, they also can deal with even more abstract ideas, such as, 'Anger and joy are both feelings', or even, 'Thinking and dreaming are both states of mind'.

In contrast, some pupils will develop abstract thinking more quickly than the typical child in their peer group. For example, at six years of age, the pupil may be able to use thinking skills usually typical of 10-year-olds. Compared with most children of the same age, this pupil will be less dependent on concrete learning and more able to use abstract thinking.

Pupils who have an advanced capacity for abstract thinking may be able to solve problems and think through situations without the need for tedious, physical calculation or practical approaches. Socially, this pupil may be a 'fish out of water,' if the pupil talks about abstract ideas that have little meaning or interest to fellow pupils.

Table 1.1 provides examples of the way thinking evolves, from ages 0–4 on through to age 15+. Although age ranges are given in the chart, it is important to remember that these ages are when this type of thinking usually begins to emerge and become possible. Older pupils (and adults) often use a combination of very basic thinking and more advanced abstract thinking. Right through to adulthood, concrete thinking plays an important part in how we deal with information.

Making connections between ideas

One of the biggest challenges in teaching is to show pupils how ideas connect to create a meaningful whole. Being able to link ideas is one of the most important aspects of learning and thinking. Some pupils find it difficult to produce a piece of work that has a coherent structure and logical flow.

Pupils with learning difficulties often seem to learn in 'boxes.' They may learn addition but not think about how it relates to subtraction. They may get help putting together a project on one topic but are unable to reapply those same skills to the next assignment.

The importance of memory

Memory is an important part of learning, and many pupils fail in school because of poor memory. There are two main types of memory.

Short-term memory is the brief storage system where information is held before it is fully processed. We 'hold' a telephone number that we have just looked up, we dial the number

Table 1.1 Developmental sequence: concrete to abstract thinking

	Typical age range	Type of thinking	Example
Level 1	0–4 years	Thought is tied to the real world and the here and now. Problem solving is often physical and not mental. Cannot think about their own thinking.	Forgets about a toy once it is hidden. Bangs on a jigsaw puzzle to make the pieces fit. Gets upset that 'tomorrow' does not happen immediately. Think that what they guess is certain to be the right answer.
Level 2	4–8 years	Thought is still closely tied to real-life experiences. Information from the senses has priority over ideas. Reasoning is often based on a single, sometimes irrelevant criterion. The child's own perspective often dominates understanding. Reasoning can be unsystematic.	Thinks that a polar bear will be 'cuddly' like their toy bear. Chooses the brightest coloured book, instead of the book that would be the most help to them in their task. Does not put peas in the vegetable category 'because peas are yucky'. Chooses a child's toy for a parent's present.
Level 3	8–15 years	Thought does not have to be tied to real life. Ability to select relevant criteria improves. Ability to coordinate more than one aspect of a problem increases. Language and thought can be used to replace action or real-life experiences. Reasoning becomes more methodical and systematic.	Can think about 'what if aliens landed' and make some reasonable assumptions. Can talk through a plan and make decisions on probable situations that might arise. Can gather several pieces of information and work it into an organised summary.
Level 4	15+ years	Thinking can be completely free of real-life experience. Ideas can be developed and thought about in a systematic way.	Can agree or disagree with other people's theories or opinions on the basis of thinking, not experience.

and then we forget it. This type of memory is fragile and can easily be disrupted. If someone speaks to us before we dial, we may have to look up the number all over again.

Long-term memory is where information is stored for later retrieval.

Moving information from short-term into long-term memory often takes conscious effort. Memory is not like a muscle, so you cannot improve memory simply by 'doing' memory tasks. The only way to improve memory is to work on the strategies that help you to store and retrieve information efficiently. These strategies include:

- paying attention
- rehearsing the information
- organising the information in chunks
- organising the information in patterns
- making sense of the information
- using memory aids (mnemonics)
- allowing enough time for learning to consolidate.

Even when information is stored in long-term memory, it is not always easily located when it is needed. We may have no recall at all, or only parts of what are needed may be recalled. Often, we have to partially reconstruct the information in order to recall the whole.

Recall is easier if:

- You knew the information or procedure thoroughly in the first place.
- You understood the information or procedure well to begin with.
- You have actively recalled the information or procedure quite frequently since it was first learned.
- You have prompts, clues or context to trigger your recall.

Recall falls into several categories.

Matching

The simplest form of memory is matching. Matching occurs when we can remember enough about one thing to say that another is the same or different. If the teacher says, 'This word is *dog*. Find me another card with the word *dog* on it', the pupil may well be able to match the word, even though they cannot read *dog* independently. (In fact, matching words is a really good beginning for reading, as you will read in Chapter 2.)

Recognition

The second form of recall is recognition. Recognition occurs when the pupil can find a given word when asked to do so e.g., 'Find the word that says *house*' even though they may not be able to read the word *house* independently.

Retrieval

The third form of memory is the retrieval of information. Retrieval is when the pupil is shown the word *because* and can draw on their memory and read it right away.

> Tess was preparing for an exam. She read her notes over and over again, until she had a comfortable feeling of familiarity. Everything she read made her confidence build. She thought, 'Yes, I know all this. There is nothing here that seems new'.
>
> If the examination had asked her to 'Check the sentences that you have read before', she would have been fine. She would have recognised every one, because she had exercised her *recognition memory* when she reviewed.
>
> However, Tess failed the exam because she had to *retrieve* information. Retrieving information is much more challenging than simply recognising it.
>
> If Tess had reviewed using active strategies such as working though previous tests, creating diagrams to organise the information and testing herself on her retrieval, she would have had a much better chance of passing.

Speed of learning

Some pupils learn slowly because they lack the foundation skills or concepts and have real difficulty mastering what is required. Their problem is not really with their *speed* of learning, but with the level of difficulty of the task..

Other pupils are quite ready to learn and capable of the task itself but simply need extra time to go through the learning process.

The speed at which a pupil learns is sometimes called a learning curve. Some pupils have a very steep learning curve. As soon as the teaching begins, they take off, and before long, they have mastered the idea and may need only a brief period of practice to consolidate the learning.

Other pupils have a more elongated learning curve. They are equally capable of succeeding with the task, but take longer to develop the ideas or skills. They may arrive at full understanding later than most. Once they get it, very little further practice may be required, or they may need to have extended practice to firm up their learning.

One of the greatest frustrations for the pupil who has a slow, gradual way of learning is that general classroom teaching is often aimed at the pupils who learn more rapidly. Often this pupil does have the capability to learn to the same level as others, provided enough instruction and practice is given.

Jack is now a successful business man, and he tells his story.

Even now, I know I need time. It's no good giving me information too fast and expecting me to take it in. I need to read it over, hear it again, think about it and then it's OK – I can handle it. Same thing at school. I never did well, never got good grades and though I liked learning, it just seemed to go too fast.

Then I had this teacher, Mr Grisham. Best thing that ever happened to me. Mr Grisham kept teaching the same thing until we knew it – no going on to the next thing until you were rock solid on the first. He wouldn't let you move an inch until he was sure you were rock solid ... and I found I could learn, really learn if we stuck at it, Mr Grisham and me.

The pupil with the extended learning curve may never get to finish any piece of new learning. Just as they are beginning to pick up, the topic is closed and the teacher moves on to the next part of the programme. As a result, the pupil may have only partial or very fragile mastery of the first topic. Often, just a few more sessions of instruction and/or practice would have been all that was needed for the pupil to really understand and master the new skill or concept.

Conversely, pupils who learn very quickly can easily get frustrated and bored if further instruction and practice is given after they have accomplished the required learning.

Language development

Without doubt, language is critically important in the process of thinking and learning. Language is the way in which we most frequently transfer information between teacher and pupil. Internal language is an important part of thinking, learning and remembering. It is hard to imagine how we would think without using words.

It follows that a pupil who finds it difficult to understand language and to use it effectively will likely have learning difficulties within the classroom. Does the pupil understand the difference between 'Draw a line down the middle of your page' and 'Draw a line to the middle of your page'? Can the pupil use words to create hypothetical situations, such as, 'If the book costs £12.00 and four people were going to buy it together, they would each have to put in _____'?

Strategies for working with individual differences

Planning for individual differences

✳ Use Appendix Form 24: 'Teacher checklist for successful learning' as a reminder of the basics of effective learning, so that all of your teaching is designed to make sure that your pupils can learn successfully.

✳ Use Appendix Form 26: 'Teacher chart for planning an inclusive programme' to look at the needs of individual pupils and to plan accordingly.

Providing for concrete and abstract thinkers

�ળ Identify the pupils in your class who work best with concrete materials and ideas. Developmentally, they may still need to work with real objects and experience hands-on learning, so provide the necessary materials.

✳ Allow pupils to use physical learning aids (such as counting on their fingers or making tally marks), if they need them. Pupils should not be made to feel that the use of these learning methods and materials is wrong.

✳ When you teach, always move from the concrete to the abstract. Start with a real-life example or demonstration of the principle you are teaching. Then move onto the more abstract ideas. For example, if you're teaching fractions, begin with real objects, then move to diagrams and finally to the written symbols.

✳ When you think pupils are ready, give explicit practice in moving from the concrete to the abstract. For instance, show the shortcut of counting on from the bigger number when adding two numbers together.

✳ Pupils who find abstract reasoning difficult often do not extract general principles from a single example, so provide several examples of the same concept. For instance, if teaching about flight, use examples of planes, birds, kites and autumn leaves to illustrate the general principles. If you use only one example, the more concrete thinkers in your class will tend to isolate the information to one example. If you use the example 'Airplanes fly because the air lifts their wings', the pupil may relate the information to airplanes but still not have any idea about what makes birds, kites or autumn leaves stay airborne.

✳ Teach pupils to think in categories as a way of enhancing their ability to use abstract rather than concrete reasoning. Classify and cross-classify items, e.g.: 'Butterflies, bees, eagles, seagulls and wasps can go into one group, because they all fly. ... Or, we could say bees and wasps go together because they can sting. ... Or, we could make one group of insects and another group of birds'.

✳ Thinking about similarities and differences also helps to develop skills in abstract thinking: 'How are a bird and an airplane alike? .... How are they different? ... What is the same about a table, a chair and a bed? ... Which is the odd one out – a bee, an eagle or a wasp? ... Which three of these pictures have something in common? ...'How many ways can we group these things?'

✳ Introduce thinking in analogies: 'Brush is to hair as broom is to ... Ceiling is to room as sky is to ...' Have pupils make their own analogies.

✳ Create a 'backward quiz,' where the pupils are given the answers, not the questions, and get them thinking in a less concrete way. For example, 'If "Africa" is the answer, what is the question?'

✳ Give true/false quizzes to stretch thinking skills. 'All bees are insects. ... All insects are bees.'

✳ Brainstorm in class various ways to develop abstract thinking. What do pupils think about questions such as: 'Why does rain fall down and not float away? .... How does hair grow?' Ask pupils to create their own questions and think about how their ideas could be tested.

Enhancing the ability to make connections between ideas

✳ Note those pupils who find it hard to see the connections between ideas, and provide them with additional, explicit instruction so they can participate equally in the classroom learning.

✳ At the start of a lesson or activity, provide plenty of background and review to prepare pupils for new learning. Let your introduction create the scene for the new learning so that all pupils can 'locate' themselves and understand the 'big picture.' This helps activate prior knowledge and establish links between old learning and new.

* Give the pupils a clear summary of what is going to be taught. Write the headings as bulleted points on the board, and work through the topic systematically. At the end of the lesson, review what has been taught by going over the bulleted points to summarise what has been covered. This helps the pupils to see how the whole lesson has been a series of connected ideas.

* Always try to link new teaching to the pupils' previous experiences. Demonstrate to pupils how what you are teaching relates to what they already know. This helps to develop the connections that, in turn, help learning to make sense.

* Make the connections between different sets of information or concepts part of your teaching. Give explicit instruction and demonstration of the links between one set of ideas and another. For example, if you are teaching subtraction in mathematics, take time to demonstrate and practice how the subtraction process relates to addition. If you are teaching about Germany, talk about the similarities and differences between Germany and Sweden (or whatever other country you have studied in class).

* Ask pupils to constantly compare and contrast new learning with previous learning: 'How is this story like the one we read last term? … How is it different?'

* Have pupils use a storyboard (a series of pictures) to create an orderly sequence of ideas.

* Use software programs designed to help organise ideas and information.

* Get pupils to draw a 'mind map' to put their ideas into a logical structure.

* Make 'recipe cards' for procedures that require logical thinking in a series of steps.

* Have a poster that gives pupils a glossary of words and phrases that help to connect ideas together: although, because, unless, even if, more than, before that, afterwards, if, when, instead of, but …

* Give explicit instruction and practice in writing sentences that combine ideas together: 'We went to the park because … I like to swim even though …'

Improving memory

* Get the pupils to pay attention to what they have to remember. Make eye contact and, if necessary, use their names.

* Alert pupils to the fact that they need to consciously attend to what they are learning: 'Now listen very carefully. You need to remember this.'

* Do not teach while a pupil is doing something else (such as finishing off previous work).

* Have pupils repeat the directions you have given them.

* Review previous learning, and check the pupils' retention.

* Have pupils over-learn information (that is learn and rehearse intensively until mastery is 100 per cent on several subsequent days). Use Appendix Form 23: 'Teacher checklist for mastery learning' to help with this.

* Support pupils who have difficulty remembering by giving them information in written form.

* Make the information interesting and appealing. Have pupils read a school notice and act out the instructions: 'Mr Saw says we have to bring the forms back tomorrow.'

* Use humour where possible to engage the pupils' interest and make the information more memorable.

* Give the information in several formats. For example, do not just tell the pupils the information verbally, but also draw a diagram or chart.

* Give pupils explicit instructions about how to store the information: 'Say it over to yourself … again … and again … and again.' (Many pupils don't realise this is necessary!)

✳ Use the example of a computer: 'Okay now, "save" that information and send it to your brain.'

✳ Take them through the rehearsal process by giving real rehearsal that you can hear or see: "'Let me see you write that over again four times. ... Tell me that same thing in six different voices. ... Let's say that through five times before playtime.'

✳ Have pupils rehearse using several senses: 'Write it down and say it over at the same time. Visualise what you have written. Whisper it to a friend.'

✳ Teach pupils to use pencil and paper, electronic organisers, computers and other memory devices to store information that is hard to remember.

✳ Give them an overview of what they have to remember: 'I'm going to tell you three things to remember. ...'

✳ Create logical patterns in the information to assist memory: "'There are six things to remember – three kinds of food and three things to wear.'

✳ Encourage visualisation: 'Imagine those six things. Three kinds of food in the basket – can you see them now? 1 ... 2 ... 3. Now three things to wear – imagine putting them on. 1 ... 2 ... 3. ... Five times six. Think about five rows of blocks, with six blocks in each row. Now imagine a big sign with 30 on the top.'

✳ Show how the information links together to make sense. 'See, you spell *today* with five letters – two little words, *to* and *day*, put together.'

✳ Have pupils use diagrams to organise information and aid recall.

✳ Put information in context so it makes sense and connects with things that are already remembered. 'Remember, we learned about how rivers erode the soil. Today we learned about two other sorts of erosion – wind erosion and ice erosion – so now we have three sorts of erosion to remember. Water, wind and ice.'

✳ Encourage pupils to create 'tricks' to help them remember, e.g., 'You *hear* with your *ear*, but *he* is in *here*.'

✳ Memory works best when there is no competition. If pupils are trying to remember something, allow some quiet time for rehearsal and consolidation before introducing new information.

✳ Build up the ability to recall specific information by giving pupils practice at matching and recognising before they have to recall. For example, ask the pupils to pair up written questions with the answer before they are asked to remember the answers independently.

✳ Get pupils to practise recalling information if they are preparing for a test or exam by using practice tests, quizzes or written assignments that will help them to retrieve information.

✳ Check how pupils are reviewing for a test or exam. Explain how reading the notes over and over may only be activating their *recognition* memory, which will not help them when they have to *recall* information in the exam. Show the pupils how to go over the information using active strategies that assist recall, such as making mind maps, writing summaries, making their own self tests, etc.

Accommodating various speeds of learning

✳ Consider those pupils in your class who are learning slowly because the task is too difficult for them to master. Provide an alternative, achievable task for those pupils you're sure are in over their heads. If you are unsure, it is a good idea to provide additional instruction and time. Perhaps the pupil *may* be able to cope with the learning given a longer exposure time.

✳ Design your teaching to accommodate pupils on the fast track, who need less instruction and practice to achieve success.

✳ Identify pupils in your class who you think *could* be expected to master the work, provided they had sufficient time and instruction. Set up your teaching to accommodate their need for more instruction, an extended period of time and/or extra practice. Continue teaching until mastery is complete.

* If pupils need additional instruction and practice, arrange for them to have supplementary work. Provide worksheets for extra practice at home, have a lunchtime study group for pupils to go over the class work, or provide additional, in-class teaching and practice sessions for those who need them.

* Vary the required finishing time for any given piece of work to allow pupils to consolidate their learning if needed..

* Instead of having a date when work is due, have an exit test to decide when the learning is complete. For example, the work will be complete when the pupil can achieve 80 per cent or more on the exit test. Pupils can take the exit test when they think they are ready to move on, and it can be repeated if necessary.

* Aim for quality, not quantity, in learning. Give the pupil fewer topics or assignments to allow them to spend more time mastering the ones they are working on.

* Avoid moving pupils on to new work unless they can demonstrate a firm grasp of what you have been teaching already.

Supporting language development

* Monitor the language you use in teaching so that pupils with difficulties can still access the information you are giving. Make clear statements, write down key points, and order and summarise what you are saying.

* Provide everyday-language versions of technical terms.

* Give clear explanation of the meanings of new words that are introduced in a subject.

* Be consistent with the vocabulary you use. For example do not switch between words such as *subtract* and *minus,* or *soluble* and *dissolves,* unless you make it clear to the pupils that you are talking about the same thing.

* If other adults (such as parents, assistants, or volunteers) are working with pupils, make sure that you all are using the same terminology.

* Make classroom charts as memory aids to help pupils assimilate new language that is being introduced.

* Supplement what you say with diagrams, graphics and demonstrations to give information in a form that pupils with language difficulties can understand.

* Provide an assistant to help pupils with language difficulties understand what is being taught.

* Allow pupils to demonstrate their learning in a variety of modes, such as drawing, drama, construction, etc., in place of spoken or written language.

* Be aware of pupils who persistently make mistakes when answering questions. They may have difficulty with the *language* of the questions rather than the underlying knowledge or concepts. Try rewording the questions or assessing their knowledge by observing them putting the concept into practice.

* Some pupils have difficulty formulating spoken or written answers, even though they understand the topic quite well. Offer alternatives, such as multiple choice answers and true/false tests.

Individual learning styles

Although learning depends to a large extent on the intrinsic capacity of the individual, personality, aptitudes and interests are important, too. Much has been written about 'multiple intelligences,' first described by Dr Howard Gardner in 1983. As teachers, our experience confirms that pupils perceive information and problems through their own, unique sets of filters. When pupils' learning styles do not match the way they are being taught, learning difficulties can very easily arise.

> It is only effective to teach by talking if you have a pupil who learns by listening

Commonly recognised learning styles include:

Verbal-linguistic intelligence (word smart)

These pupils like to listen and to talk, read and write.

Interpersonal intelligence (people smart)

Group dynamics and person-to-person relationships are priorities for these pupils.

Kinesthetic intelligence (body smart)

Physical activity, tactile sensation and movement are important to these pupils.

Naturalist intelligence (nature smart)

These pupils are very in tune with the natural world around them.

Musical, rhythmic intelligence (music smart)

Music and rhythm have meaning and appeal to these pupils.

Intrapersonal intelligence (self smart)

These pupils show independent thinking and action and highly developed self-awareness.

Spatial intelligence (picture smart)

Patterns, graphics, drawing and construction are strong learning channels for these pupils.

Logical mathematical intelligence (mathematics smart)

These pupils like logic, mathematical order and systems.

Aesthetic intelligence (beauty smart)

Sensory beauty (colours, shapes, textures, perfumes) have a strong appeal to these pupils.

Strategies for working with individual learning styles

✱ Plan your teaching and assessments to utilise the pupil's preferred way of learning.
✱ Offer alternatives so that pupils with different learning styles can work in the way that suits them best within the same curriculum area.

    For example, pupils might all study the same geography topic but take different angles depending on their learning styles. The pupils with highly developed interpersonal intelligence might work on the social aspects of the district they are studying; the logical, mathematical pupils might collect data and statistics; spatially aware pupils could draw maps and build models; while other pupils might focus on the flora and fauna and weather systems.

✱ *Verbal-linguistic intelligence.* These pupils thrive in a traditional classroom where most of the teaching and learning is based on spoken and written language. These pupils may prefer to learn by reading, talking and thinking rather than through practical activities. They may like to use words and language creatively in stories, poetry or drama.

* *Interpersonal intelligence.* These pupils learn best when they are able to work in groups, share ideas and support each other. They may find it difficult to connect with abstract or theoretical learning. They will be more involved if there is a human interest component in the topic. For example, they may not be interested in mathematics for its own sake but become very involved when working out mathematics connected with social situations, such as fundraising for a good cause.

* *Kinesthetic intelligence.* These pupils may find sitting still in class very difficult and may need frequent opportunities to move around. They may learn best through practical, active learning. They may be talented at sports, dance and other physical activities.

* *Naturalist intelligence.* These pupils will learn most effectively when they can connect with the living world. They may find being indoors frustrating and much prefer to be outside. Their preferred reading and viewing is often factual (documentaries) rather than fiction. They may connect well with hands-on activities that involve the natural world.

* *Musical, rhythmic intelligence.* These pupils may be very sensitive to noise and be disturbed by unpleasant sounds, such as loud, harsh or high-pitched voices, background noises, such as air conditioners, or competing sounds, such as noise from the class next door.

   Using music in their general classroom programme may enhance their involvement. They may have a strong need for musical or rhythmic expression and may need a legitimate outlet for this, such as being part of a choir, band or orchestra or being a solo performer.

* *Intrapersonal intelligence.* These pupils may actively dislike group work and prefer to work alone. They may prefer tasks where they are asked to give their own views and develop their own ideas independently. They may have distinct personal opinions and be prepared to defend their own ideas. They may like situations where they can negotiate what is required of them rather than having to follow the rules exactly.

* *Spatial intelligence.* When learning can be approached through graphics, design, visual patterns, construction and the like, these pupils usually enjoy learning. These pupils may prefer practical subjects, such as art, craft, design, technology and mechanics.

* *Logical mathematical intelligence.* These pupils obviously enjoy mathematics and orderly sequenced learning. Scientific enquiry, research and information technology may have strong appeal. They may find creative tasks, where imagination or expressive, creative language is required, more difficult to master.

* *Aesthetic intelligence.* Pupils with high aesthetic intelligence are very aware of sensory information. They will notice presentation of learning materials and enjoy books, worksheets and equipment that have an aesthetic appeal. They may dislike having to work with materials that are ugly or unpleasant to look at or touch.

Characteristics of a good learner

Learning characteristics make a big difference to learning outcomes. Some pupils find learning very easy. Some pupils find learning difficult and may have special needs. However, the individual pupils' characteristics as learners (curious or apathetic, persistent or easily defeated, overly cautious or willing to take sensible risks and so on) will make a very significant difference to the quality of their learning.

Significant learning difficulties can be outweighed by strengths in persistence, curiosity, risk taking and so on. The characteristics of a good learner will go a long way towards making sure that the pupil is fully integrated and included within the classroom, despite the fact that the pupil experiences some significant difficulties with learning.

Conversely, high ability can be negated by negative learning characteristics, such as apathy towards new ideas, poor self-reflection and lack of persistence.

Some pupils in your class may be passive consumers of television and computer entertainment and not have had opportunities to develop their natural curiosity or their capacity for flexible thinking. Others may want instant results and give up too fast when success does not come quickly. Yet again, some pupils may be so afraid of making a mistake that they will try only things they are certain of getting right. Such pupils' learning difficulties may relate more to their characteristics as learners than to any problems they may have with the learning process itself.

Many notable discoveries have been made by scientists who were no more intelligent or better qualified than their peers. Some succeeded because they were more persistent, others because they were more prepared to think flexibly or follow the lead of their natural curiosity. Some scientists have made brilliant discoveries that were confined to their laboratories until someone with better communication skills came along.

Addressing your pupils' learning characteristics and working towards positive qualities is an important part of inclusion and intervention for all pupils, but especially for those who are already challenged by finding some aspects of learning difficult.

Strategies for developing good learners

Stimulating curiosity and enthusiasm for knowledge

✱ Pupils with learning difficulties often seem to have little energy left over to be curious or enjoy learning for its own sake. Identify any of your pupils who lack curiosity or zest for learning. Plan to stimulate this important characteristic in these pupils as an important foundation for learning. Ask questions and bring in exciting or interesting resources to get the pupils interested and intrigued.

✱ Show your own enthusiasm for information. Express your own curiosity. Share your knowledge and let your pupils see that there is an endless and exciting range of things to learn about. Welcome questions and discussions.

✱ Give many opportunities for real-life, practical science. Explore your local environment, experiment in the classroom and try things out to find answers.

✱ Give assignments that encourage research and exploration for new information.

✱ Team a pupil who seems to lack curiosity with a partner who can model willingness to explore and go beyond the basic task.

✱ Subscribe to science or nature magazines that stimulate your pupils' curiosity and interest in the world around them.

✱ Encourage pupils to become questioners and to find out the answers. Make sure your classroom has a good stack of attractive reference books. Change the books regularly to create new interest.

✱ Allocate class time for pupils to browse through interesting books, magazines and other resources. Encourage them to follow through on their own interests.

✱ Use interesting posters and displays, and change them often to introduce new ideas and information into your classroom.

✱ Have pupils create a class quiz on a wide range of chosen topics, such as insects, life in our town in the 1950s, South American animals, the human body, automobiles, the solar system and so on. Every pupil contributes at least one question (and has the answer to that question worked out).

✱ Ask pupils with special interests to follow them up in depth. Vary assignments to accommodate a special interest.

✱ Encourage pupils to set up their own interest groups or clubs. Perhaps arrange for a special place for meetings at recess and lunch breaks. They can make collections and 'museum' displays for the interest of others. They might collect rocks as a geology group, collect information about aircraft or start a gardening club. The possibilities are endless.

✱ Have general knowledge quizzes at regular intervals in your class.

✱ Encourage an interest in words and their meanings. Get pupils to research word meanings and the origin of words and sayings.

* Have pupils research the meaning of their own names.
* Get pupils to find out about their own family history by talking to their parents, grandparents, aunts and uncles.

Encouraging flexible thinking

* Pupils with learning difficulties may find flexible thinking difficult. Notice those pupils in your class who rely on *remembering* what they have been taught, rather than producing new ideas. Plan to encourage these pupils to think by presenting questions that have to be worked out by thinking.
* Introduce puzzles that use visual sequences or codes to encourage thinking in logical sequences.
* Have fun with 'what if' ideas: 'What if it rained soup? ... What if you could fly? ... What if time went backwards?'
* Introduce Venn diagrams to encourage pupils to classify and cross-classify their ideas.
* Use the *Six Thinking Hats* technique devised by author Edward de Bono to show pupils how to use thinking skills flexibly. With this technique, each hat colour signifies a different style of thinking. This technique helps pupils to change their patterns of thinking. The pupil who frequently is a Red Hat thinker (intuitive process) may be asked to use White Hat thinking (using facts and figures). If the class devises a plan that everyone in class is enthusiastic to implement, pupils may be asked to put on Black Hats to be sure they have not overlooked potential problems. If the class becomes stuck on a problem, they may be asked to put on Blue Hats and think about how to move forward.

  White Hat: Focus on the facts that you already have; look for gaps in the information.
  Red Hat: Look at the problem using your intuition and 'gut feeling.' Think about how other people will respond.
  Black Hat: Look at all the negatives; look cautiously and defensively. Look for the problems.
  Yellow Hat: Look positively and on the optimistic side.
  Green Hat: Think creatively. Use your imagination.
  Blue Hat: Control the process of thinking and problem-solving. Decide what strategies to use.

* Ask for flexible thinking in your classroom: 'What could we use instead of a ruler for this job? ... Let's think of a different way of getting to the playground.'
* Value the diversity of ideas in your classroom. Always welcome different ideas, and be prepared to discuss the range of ideas that come from the class. Do not allow pupils to ridicule ideas that are suggested by others.
* When you brainstorm ideas with the class, write every idea up on the board. Show how even 'wrong' ideas can give information that helps to solve the problem: 'At first we thought we could use a paper bag. That was no good, though, because when it got wet, it fell to pieces. So we knew we needed something that stayed strong when it got wet.'
* Collect riddles and encourage pupils to make up their own.
* Get pupils to do crossword puzzles and other word puzzles.

Pushing persistence and determination

* Many pupils who find learning difficult become discouraged. Look at the pupils in your class and identify those who seem to lack persistence and determination. Plan to work on these important learning characteristics with those pupils.
* Use Appendix Form 30: 'Pupil guide to making changes' to help pupils clarify where extra effort is needed.

✳   Avoid letting pupils leave work unfinished, as this develops a poor work ethic.

✳   Use flexible time limits so that work can be completed, even if it takes the pupil longer than others.

✳   Be honest with pupils, and when a task is challenging, tell them that it will need a high level of persistence. Celebrate when they succeed.

✳   Give tasks difficulty ratings. Give bonus points for tasks with high difficulty ratings: 'This task has a difficulty rating of nine, which means it's a tough one. You'll get a bonus of nine points for giving it a try, and then a maximum of five points for getting all five questions right. Or, you can try this one, which is easier and rated two, so you get two points and then a maximum of five points.'

✳   Give pupils credit and public recognition of persistence and determination as a valued learning characteristic: 'We can be so proud of Jess. It took her four tries to get her story the way she wanted it – but she did it!'

✳   Help pupils to set personal goals and reward their achievement. Use Appendix Form 33: 'Pupil guide to setting goals' to help with this.

✳   Encourage self-talk and self-motivation to enhance persistence and determination. Have pupils tell themselves they can succeed, or have them make motivational notes to put on their desks.

✳   Collect and value stories of children and adults who have shown determination in the face of difficulties and use them as role models.

✳   Work with the idea of practice, training and application being important elements in success. Emphasise the way in which successful sports men and women put in many hours of training and practice to reach their goals.

✳   Show pupils that setbacks and failures are part of the process of success. Talk the pupils through difficult patches by showing them how they are gradually building up to eventual success.

Fostering good communication

✳   Communication involves good listening. Encourage your pupils to be attentive listeners by making your teaching dynamic and involving. Expect your pupils to interact with you as you teach. Ask questions, invite ideas and foster active involvement.

✳   Model good listening. Teach your pupils about eye contact, taking turns when speaking and keeping to the topic of conversation.

✳   Provide experience in structuring communication so it makes sense. Pupils need to organise ideas into a logical sequence. They need to make clear statements at the beginning and the end of what they say, so the listener has a framework for what they hear. Have them prepare talks using prompt cards, numbering each card so their plan has a sequence.

✳   Try having the pupils role-play TV newscasts to get them thinking about telling a story in a clear and engaging way.

✳   Look at professional broadcasters. Ask the pupils to identify how these people make their communication clear to the listeners.

✳   Most professional communicators have an editor, producer or director to enhance what they do. Offer pupils the same support. Have an adult or fellow pupil take on the role of editor, producer or director when the pupil is preparing a presentation or speech. That person's role can be acknowledged: 'I would like to thank my producer, Tim Atkins, who worked with me on this presentation'. Or 'Written by Frankie Khan, edited by Rosa Patagonis'.

✳   Give all pupils the chance to communicate with a range of audiences, such as the whole class, a group of younger pupils or visitors to the school. Give every pupil in your class an equal opportunity to take on roles such as showing visitors around the school and speaking in front of the class. If the pupil does not have the necessary skills, rehearse what is required.

✳ Some pupils will have difficulties in specific areas, such as writing, talking, etc. They may be able to get their ideas across using art, graphics, computer programs, drama, construction or demonstration.

✳ Keeping to the topic is an important part of good communication. Provide activities in which pupils have to sift out irrelevant information from a talk or reading passage.

✳ Answering questions exactly is another important part of good communication. Pupils often think long answers are always better than short answers. Let them discover that a good answer is one that relates exactly to the question that is asked. Give them a question and then sort out possible answers. Ask 'Which answers were the best ?'

✳ Have the pupils rewrite long messages in as few words as possible to get them to communicate the essential facts clearly.

Encouraging sensible risk-taking

✳ Many pupils with learning difficulties do not like to take risks, because they so often make mistakes. Make sure tasks are at the right level, with sufficient support, so there is only a small risk of making a mistake and a high chance of getting things right.

✳ Some pupils think that getting something right is the only thing that counts. Always emphasise that making an attempt is an achievement in itself, regardless of the outcome: "That was a great try. … You gave that your best shot. … That was tough, and you nearly cracked the first part.'

✳ Show pupils ways of saying they are not certain: 'My guess is that … it could be … I am not sure, but I think that … maybe … perhaps … my hunch is … I don't think this is right, but I'll have a try.'

✳ Tell stories of people who have taken on challenges and tried, often again and again, to succeed. Many scientists and explorers only made breakthrough discoveries by taking some chances.

Supporting self-reflection

✳ Use Appendix Form 36: 'Pupil: what I think about school' to help pupils identify their own learning profile and feelings about learning.

✳ Pupils with learning difficulties often fail to evaluate their own work. They may be passive learners, waiting to hear how they have done from the teacher. Encourage your pupils to evaluate their own learning ahead of teacher response. You can use the Appendix Form 35: 'Pupil: self-evaluation' to help your pupils reflect on their own learning.

✳ Before evaluating pupil work, ask them to talk you through what they have done. Explore their thinking behind their work. Why did they decide on that topic? Would they make the same choice now? How did they find their information? Were there other sources they could have tried?

✳ Encourage pupils to take an active rather than passive role in meetings regarding their programmes. Give pupils the Appendix Form 39: 'Pupil notes: getting ready for a meeting' to help them prepare.

Self-esteem, self-confidence and optimism

Self-esteem is the value that you place on yourself. If you lack self-esteem, you may:

• assume that other people do not like or value you
• disbelieve any positives that people say about you

- feel uncomfortable with praise or success
- be easily led and afraid to trust your own judgement
- not feel entitled to fair or equal treatment
- be defensive if people try to help you.

Self-confidence has to do with your belief in your ability to succeed. If you lack self-confidence, you may:

- expect to fail at a particular task
- be low in motivation because you do not expect to succeed
- find it hard to overcome setbacks, because you think that proves you have failed.

Optimism is the belief that things will turn out well. If you lack optimism, then you may:

- be certain that things will go badly, even before you have begun
- notice the negatives more than the positives
- place negative interpretations on the daily ups and downs of life
- see reasons why things will go wrong more easily than reasons why things will go well.

Inclusion is a two-way street, and pupils themselves are an important part of the process. Of course the *community* has to believe in the principle of inclusion and have inclusive systems and strategies put in place. However, that is only half of the story. The *pupils* have to have enough self-esteem, self-confidence and optimism to believe in their own entitlement to equal opportunities. Without this sense of entitlement, they will not be able to accept and utilise the inclusive practices that are available.

Steve has multiple difficulties in school. He thinks that because he is different, he is inferior. He assumes that his future prospects are bleak. Steve thinks that the strategies offered to him are 'a waste of time', because he 'knows' that he can never succeed or overcome his difficulties. He does not feel that he is worth the effort that people put in. He expects to disappoint those who work with him. Steve does not cooperate with his teachers or with the services and support that they provide.

Jamal also has multiple difficulties in school. He has good self-esteem and values his own, unique set of characteristics. He has a strong sense of entitlement to inclusive strategies that are offered and a high expectation that, working with his teachers, he will be able to reach his full potential. Jamal believes that the inclusion program is his right and uses the opportunities to their fullest extent.

Strategies for building self-esteem, self-confidence and optimism

Boosting self-esteem

✱ Provide the pupil's inclusive provisions as rights not privileges. Deal with difficulties honestly and with an open approach.
✱ Build a warm and personal relationship with the pupil. This seems very obvious, but it is all too easily forgotten.
✱ Take time to listen attentively, with enthusiasm, sympathy or whatever is appropriate.
✱ Make positive eye contact.
✱ Refer to what the pupil has previously told you about herself: 'How's that new dog of yours doing, Marcia?'

✳ Smile at the pupil – for real.

✳ Greet the pupil warmly – with heart.

✳ Share something about yourself with the pupil.

✳ Find points of similarity and connection between yourself and the pupil – the same pet, the same favorite colour, mutual interests or favors: 'Let's hope our team wins on Saturday, John. ... Cheri, could I borrow your pen for a minute? ... I'll bring that book in from home to show you.'

✳ Ask for information or advice from the pupil where you know they have expertise or knowledge: 'My friends are coming over this weekend. Do you know a good place for their kids to skateboard?'

✳ Be honest with both praise and criticism, so the pupil trusts your opinion.

✳ Show respect for the pupil's ideas and feelings: 'What do you think about that? ... How do you feel that would work? ... I agree with you; that's a good idea. You go ahead and get started. ... Should we do it in red? Or maybe blue would be better. What do you think?''

✳ Have high expectations of the pupil: 'I know I can trust you with that. You are responsible.'

✳ Encourage the pupils to acknowledge their profiles of strength: 'You know you are good at sticking to the task. ... You are such a friendly person.'

✳ Teach pupils to evaluate their own efforts and to give themselves credit when they know they have done a good job. Similarly, teach them to be honest with themselves, so they do not accept second best from themselves.

✳ Remind the pupils that they are each unique. 'There is only one me in this world, and only one Josh Neilson, and only one Cilla DeMaggio. No one else even comes close!'

✳ Use Appendix Form 37: 'Pupil reward cards' to provide positive messages about the pupils' behaviour and attitudes.

Strengthening self-confidence

✳ Set tasks with a realistic level of challenge, so pupils can take pride in achievements.

✳ Give feedback about personal qualities as well as competitive achievements: 'You are such a kind kid. ... Your smile makes my day. ... I love the way you give everything a try.'

✳ Encourage pupils to showcase their achievements for instance taking pieces of work home or showing the principal what they have done.

✳ Show the pupil that making a good attempt is, in itself, a success. The outcome is less important: 'That was a really good effort. ... You had some good ideas about how to tackle the task.'

✳ Show confidence in the pupil yourself: 'I bet you will give this a really good shot.'

✳ Give pupils choices about the level of difficulty they want to tackle. Give them opportunities to try out more difficult tasks once they have gained confidence at their starting point.

✳ Use Appendix Form 38: 'Pupil guide to "I can do"' to help pupils think positively.

Encouraging optimism

✳ Encourage pupils to plan for positive outcomes and to think their way around potential difficulties.

✳ Teach pupils to discriminate between problems in the here and now (which do need to be dealt with) and hypothetical problems in the future, which may never happen.

✳ Encourage positive thinking. If pupils are predicting 'worst-case scenarios', get them to balance these with 'best-case scenarios'.

* Encourage problem solving, so the pupils learn that whatever might happen in the future (good or bad), there is usually a way to deal with it.
* Model optimism. Be positive and confident about the future yourself.
* Challenge catastrophic language used by the pupil and others. 'Would it really be a "disaster" or just a bit of a nuisance?"'
* Use humour to defuse negative experiences or expectations and put them in perspective.

The inclusive classroom

Being included in a group and *feeling* included can be two, quite different situations. We have probably all been in situations where we have felt as if we were outsiders, even when we have been invited or have an absolute right to be part of a particular group.

If the pupil feels that they do not really belong to the class, then inclusion has not really happened. Often the pupil with difficulties or differences feels marginalised or excluded from the social group, even when the teacher uses a wide range of appropriate inclusive teaching strategies. These inclusive strategies are unlikely to work well if they are given in a context where the pupil *feels* socially excluded. Once again, remember that often it is not *what* you do, but *how* you do it.

> The teacher says 'Good work' to us … like she's trying to make us feel better about being dumb.
> All of us bad readers get 'Good Reader' badges.

Strategies for creating an inclusive classroom

* Create a class identity where everyone belongs. Have a class name, motto, badge, colour, code word, flag, song or anything else that marks *every* pupil as a rightful member of the group.
* Do things together as a class, organise a show for the rest of the school, go on a field trip, do community service or anything that involves *everyone* in the class on an equal footing.
* Refer to the class as a group: 'All of us in Room 3 … We all want to … We look out for each other in the playground. …'
* Monitor how you deal with the pupils in your class. Do you have a 'special' voice or phrase that you use only with the pupils with special needs? If so, revise your style!
* Make sure that all pupils have equal responsibilities. You may need to modify how they meet their responsibilities, but this does not mean they are excused from them. For example, everyone has an equal responsibility to keep the classroom tidy. The pupil who uses a wheelchair may have different duties from the other pupils but still does his or her fair share of the work.
* Make sure that every pupil has equal opportunities. For example, if your class has a pupil representative, then every pupil is equally eligible to be chosen. Provide support and assistance if needed, so the pupil can meet the obligations.
* Make class rules that are inclusive, so everyone can keep them. For example, if a class has a pupil with autism who often calls out, the class rules might be adjusted: 'Listen quietly when the teacher is speaking or go to the quiet corner with Mrs K.' The same rule applies to every pupil.
* Work with the whole class to look at inclusive strategies in play and socialisation: 'How can you adapt the rules of the game so that everyone can join in? … What if one of us has no one to play with at breaktime? … Some pupils will need a friend for this game.'

✳ Teach pupils to value diversity and individual differences by valuing them yourself: 'It's so interesting how you all thought of different ideas. … It's never boring with this group. … So many different people, all with something special.'

✳ Invite a range of guests into your class to speak to the pupils, so they can see that everyone has an amazing array of talents: 'Jack's father can bake bread and do ballroom dancing, Lilla's mother can drive a truck and mend a car, and Sam's sister wears really interesting clothes and draws great pictures.'

✳ Use real-life stories to highlight the fact that many people with apparent disadvantages do exceptional things.

✳ Intervention and inclusive practices should be an integral part of what you do, not an 'add on' or extra to 'normal' work. Reflect this in the way in which you plan, talk and write about your program. For example:

'We will all be studying frogs this week, and you will all have your own tasks to complete. You can find your task in the tray with your name.' This is inclusive. Everyone has his or her own task to do.

Instead of:

'We will all be studying frogs this week. Everyone will be doing the task that I have written on the board. Marcia and Cedda, you have your own special tasks to do on frogs.' This is not inclusive. Marcia and Cedda are not doing the 'real' work like the rest of the pupils. They have something different to do. Therefore, they are not included in 'everyone'.

Concluding Chapter 1

This chapter has presented numerous strategies for effective teaching and for creating and enhancing an inclusive educational environment. The variety of capabilities, skills, and learning styles that are inherent in any group of children can be a challenge. Intervention and flexibility are necessary to adjust teaching styles to the variety of levels, speeds and styles of learning encountered in the classroom – but it can be done! The specific ideas suggested here will help you to make every pupil feel welcome and a part of the group and help you to build on every child's strengths.

Remember, inclusion is first and foremost an attitude and approach that needs to be adopted in the entire school community to be most effective. As a teacher and one of the leaders of your community, you can provide a model of and support for this attitude and approach, making your school a happier place, where all children can achieve their personal potentials.

Chapter 2

Reading

Introduction

We all know reading is an important life skill. Many children acquire reading skills easily. In a world where print is so important, these fortunate pupils are well equipped. They can use reading to learn and to gain information from the world around them. Reading can enhance their lives and be a source of great pleasure.

But what of the 15 per cent or so of pupils who find reading difficult? In class, the pupil may experience a considerable disadvantage because of inaccurate or slow reading. Significant emotional and motivational challenges also may arise for the pupil who is struggling with such a fundamentally important skill.

For pupils with reading difficulties, intervention in school is vitally important to help develop their reading skills and minimise the risk of long-term disadvantages. Within the classroom, a wide range of modifications will also be needed to make sure that the pupils with reading difficulties can participate to the fullest extent.

The main subjects in this chapter follow the structure of the Appendix Form 1: 'Reading observation chart'. The chart is divided into 11 sections, each focusing on a specific area of reading. The reading observation chart may be reproduced and used to informally assess and record individual reading difficulties for pupils. As you assess individual pupils, specific patterns of difficulty may emerge. The sections in the reading observation chart will provide a direct link between the recordings in the chart and the corresponding sections in this chapter that provide strategies to help the pupil in those specific area(s) of need.

The 11 sections of the chart have also been reproduced within the main text of this chapter. If you are interested in using the strategies without completing an informal assessment of the pupil, these sections will easily guide you through the chapter and provide a quick and easy reference tool for specific areas in reading. This will enable you to select from the intervention strategies, modifications and adaptations listed to help individuals and small groups of pupils.

The following forms from the Appendix are referred to in this chapter:

Appendix Form 1:   'Reading observation chart'
Appendix Form 40: 'Parent guide to reading at home'
Appendix Form 38: 'Pupil guide to "I can do"'
Appendix Form 33: 'Pupil guide to setting goals'
Appendix Form 23: 'Teacher checklist for mastery learning'
Appendix Form 8:   '100 minutes reading chart'
Appendix Form 6:   'Diagnostic phonics assessment'
Appendix Form 5:   '100 most frequently used words'.

The first section provides an understanding of and strategies for dealing with general negativity towards reading.

Pupil feels negative about reading

Reading observation chart: section 1

1 Pupil feels negative about reading

Pupil is reluctant to read; will not read without prompting; complains when reading

Pupil avoids reading, 'loses' book, tries delaying tactics

Pupil becomes angry or upset with reading

Pupil tries to avoid reading in front of fellow pupils

When we consider how important reading is within the classroom and everyday life, it is not surprising that pupils who find reading difficult often become embarrassed, frustrated, distraught or angry. Reading is a highly complex skill, and some pupils, even if they are intelligent and motivated, truly find the process very difficult.

Pupils with reading difficulties may be afraid that adults will be angry or disappointed with them. Adults do sometimes show irritation or frustration when a pupil stumbles through what seems to be easy reading or makes the same mistake over and over again. It is easy for adults to think that the pupil simply needs to put in more effort.

> The parent or teacher may be thinking:
> 'If only he would try harder. … He can't be trying if he makes so many mistakes. … I can't believe how many times he has forgotten this word.'
> On the other hand, the pupil may also be feeling very frustrated and anxious:
> 'I can tell Mum is getting mad at me. … I am trying as hard as I can. … This is so tough to do. … It all looks the same to me… . Why can't I get this? … I've forgotten it all over again!'

The pupil may be afraid that having difficulties with reading means they are 'dumb'. It is hard to believe in yourself if you can't read well, especially when most of your peers seem to be coping so easily. The possibility of ridicule from classmates can be a very real fear.

- What will the other kids say if they see I am reading a little kid's book?
- Will they laugh at me when I make a mistake reading in front of the class?
- Will they think I'm dumb if I get special help?

Once a pupil is anxious, defensive or angry about reading, then the teacher has a much harder task in addressing not only the reading difficulties but also the negativity towards reading that has developed.

Strategies for developing positive attitudes towards reading

Communicating with all teachers

✱ All teachers need to be made aware of the pupil's difficulties with reading. The teachers also need clear and concise information about what special provisions have been agreed to, such as modified assignments, tests read aloud, audiotapes of reading material, etc. For pupils who receive special education services, these will be documented in the Individual Education Plan (IEP).

✱ In some large schools, it is difficult to stay in contact with every teacher. The pupil can be provided with a laminated card that states that the pupil has reading difficulties and itemises the special modifications that are required. This card can be discreetly shown to any teacher as needed.

* When pupils transfer from one year level to the next or change schools, information about strategies that have been used successfully should be passed on to the new teacher before the pupil begins in the new class.

Giving parents support

* Talk to the pupil's parents to ensure that they are being supportive. Some parents find it hard to understand their child's reading difficulties and may let their own frustration show.
* Parents need to know that reading is a complex skill and that reading difficulties are not unusual, even in bright, motivated pupils.
* Be aware that some parents may themselves have reading difficulties and find it difficult to support the pupil. In this case, arrange for alternative support in the school or community.
* Give the parents help with supporting reading and building confidence. You can use the parent information sheet Appendix Form 40: 'Parent guide to reading at home'.

Respecting the pupil's self-esteem

* Respect the pupils' sensitivities about their reading difficulties. Some pupils are self-conscious about being excluded from reading in front of the class, even though they are anxious about making mistakes. Check with the pupils to see whether or not they are comfortable reading in front of the class.
* If the pupil chooses to read in front of the class, you can arrange to give the pupil prior warning so he or she can rehearse the reading ahead of time. Help the pupil prepare if necessary.
* If the pupil chooses not to read in front of the class, deal with this tactfully.
* Teachers will be strong role models in showing the class as a whole that pupils with reading difficulties are accepted and supported without criticism, put-downs or ridicule.
* If the pupil's programme plan involves the pupil receiving support that is obvious to fellow pupils (for example, if the reading specialist visits the pupil in the classroom or if the pupil leaves the classroom for special support), be particularly careful that this is handled sensitively. Talk to the pupil about what type of help he or she feels most comfortable having.
* Provide all pupils with information about individual differences. Seek out examples of successful adults who struggled with reading difficulties and introduce your class to their stories. Examples that you could provide include Tom Cruise, Whoopi Goldberg, Pablo Picasso, Thomas Edison and Leonardo Da Vinci.
* Ask a colleague, parent, pupil or well-known community member who has reading difficulties to talk to the class, so everyone understands that reading difficulties are part of life and can be managed successfully.
* Provide the pupil with honest information and supportive counselling. Talk honestly about the reading difficulties and reassure the pupil that this does not mean they are dumb. Explain that, like many complex skills, reading can take time to master, and that many very smart and successful people had reading difficulties when they were pupils and may still have.
* Give objective, quantified information about the pupil's reading abilities. Reassure the pupil that they will be able to make progress and will be given the necessary support.
* Give objective, quantified information about the pupil's strengths to counterbalance the information about their reading difficulties.

* Use the Appendix Form 38: 'Pupil guide to "I can do"' worksheet to help pupils come to terms with their learning difficulties.
* Pupils may need ongoing counselling and support to understand that, with effort, appropriate help and perseverance, their reading will improve.
* Create a positive and personal relationship with pupils who require extra help with reading. If possible, maintain continuity of help if things are going well.
* Be prepared to change the approach, setting or teacher if the pupil becomes or remains negative about reading. A poor attitude from the pupil indicates that the modifications already created are not effective in dealing with the interplay of reading difficulties and frustration/low confidence.
* Remember that trying to bolster confidence by excessive praise is not helpful. Pupils soon become cynical about praise that is won too easily or is not honest. The pupil with reading difficulties may simply feel patronised when an adult praises them.

> That was a really easy book for most kids in my class, so she must think I'm dumb if she thought my reading was fantastic. ... I know she's only saying that to make me feel good. ... She says that stuff about 'fantastic reading' to all the kids who can't read. She never says it to good readers.

* Praise needs to be genuine to be effective. Praise the effort, persistence, courage and determination the pupil shows in tackling the difficult task of reading.
* Give honest feedback about the pupil's reading, so the pupil values compliments when they are given. (But make sure the reading tasks you give the pupil are appropriate, so you can give honest praise for real successes.)
* Pupils often need to see tangible evidence of real positives before they can truly believe they are progressing. Keep good records of reading progress, and share these with the pupils so they can see for themselves the progress being made.
* If there are good role models within your school, community or the pupil's family, ask them to mentor the pupil and show that even though reading can be hard, the difficulties can be managed and success achieved.
* Provide pupils who have reading difficulties with opportunities to show their strengths in academic, athletic, musical, interpersonal, artistic or community-based areas of interest.
* Provide positive affirmation by assigning the pupil special responsibilities or positions that add status in the school community despite reading problems.
* If necessary, provide the pupil with administrative help. For example, a pupil chosen as class leaser or class representative could be asked to select a fellow pupil to act as secretary to the captain to assist with reading tasks.
* Publicly recognise the pupil's successes by celebrating such milestones as 'most improved in word decoding', 'personal best in reading word list', or 'ahead of schedule in reading programme'. Emphasise effort and give credit for perseverance.
* Include the pupil as part of the intervention process. Talk to the pupil about how you are going to work together to deal with the reading difficulties the pupil is experiencing. Show the pupil your record of the skills that have already been mastered. Follow through with a clear programme of intervention, so the pupil can see how your programme will take them step by step through the stages of learning to read.
* If the pupil is self-conscious about being seen with 'little kids" books, allow them to have two reading books on their desk. One book is for image and is typical of the books that other pupils are reading. Perhaps the pupil can listen to this book on tape or see a video of the story, if available. The second book is more appropriate for the pupil's reading level. This book must still be chosen to match the pupil's age and interest levels. A wide variety of high interest–low vocabulary reading books are available for the older pupil.

✳ If a pupil wants to read aloud to the class, allow time for rehearsal. Let the pupil decide how to prepare for their 'performance'. This could include private, silent reading, listening to an adult reading the passage and/or reading aloud to a helpful adult. The pupil could also read along with an audiotape as often as required. Allow extra time to rehearse the difficult parts until the pupil is confident and ready to read in front of the group.

✳ Let the pupils choose when they are ready to read the book to an audience. In this manner, the pupils are not pressured to read without assistance until they feel sufficiently confident and well prepared to give it a try.

✳ You may be able to allow the pupil to choose who they will read to. Perhaps the pupil will read it onto a tape or read to a grandparent or a school friend.

✳ Although, as the professional educator, you will need to design the overall programme, allow the pupil to make some choices in what to learn and how. Ask the pupil to make some choices within the teaching goals that you have identified. 'Next we have to study the "oa" and "ai" sounds. Which shall we do first?'

Pupil is disadvantaged by poor reading

Reading observation chart: section 2

---

2. Pupil is disadvantaged by poor reading

Pupil demonstrates difficulty reading materials or textbooks suitable for age group

Pupil needs additional time to complete reading tasks compared to peers

Pupil does not finish reading assignments in the allotted time

Pupil runs out of time in examinations because of slow reading

---

Pupils with reading difficulties are often substantially disadvantaged with school work. Information they can easily understand if it is spoken may be a mystery to them if it is presented in print. This means that they may not be able to learn at the same rate and level as their classmates, even though they have similar intelligence.

Researching a topic is very difficult when reading is slow and inaccurate. The pupil will not be able to scan through possible reference books to decide which ones offer the best information for a project. Just reading a few pages of one book may take hours and discourage the pupil right from the beginning. The pupil may not have time to read several complementary texts and therefore have to rely on the first one selected, regardless of its merit.

Some pupils spend an enormous amount of time and effort trying to keep up with the reading requirements, although this commitment may not show in their results.

> I spend hours and hours reading, even on weekends. It takes me forever to get through just one or two chapters! But the teachers always say, 'More time spent reading would improve her results.'

When researching information on the Internet, the pupils with reading difficulties may become overloaded with too much information. The pupil may have trouble sifting through the numerous pages to find the key pieces of information. As a result, the pupil may resort to simply copying and pasting sections of information without much thought.

In tests and examinations, pupils with reading difficulties may misread questions. This can lead to the loss of many valuable points.

> A very smart adult taking a real estate agents' examination lost 25 per cent of his points because she wrote about 'unfinished' apartments instead of 'unfurnished' apartments!

Pupils may also read so slowly that they spend much of the available time reading the questions, leaving only limited time in which to write their answers. It is often a warning sign of reading difficulties when a capable pupil, who does well with classwork and homework, constantly submits work that is incomplete when done as a timed test or examination.

Slow readers may miss out on part of the reading assignments. For instance, if the teacher asks the class to read three chapters of the class novel before Friday, the pupil who reads slowly may only be able to finish one or two chapters, even if they put in a fair amount of effort. This means, of course, that this pupil also misses out on important information. If the class is reading a novel, then the pupil may lose the continuity of the story, because several chapters are skipped at intervals throughout the book.

Strategies for managing the disadvantages of poor reading

Using inclusive strategies

* Make inclusiveness a priority. Some bright pupils have reading difficulties, which may mask their underlying capabilities. Pupils who have the intelligence to learn a particular subject will need teachers to make special arrangements and modifications in the classroom so that they have an appropriate programme of academic study.
* Create resource packs to support the pupil with lessons and projects. The packs should contain selected reference articles, highlighted text and condensed information related to given topics.
* Provide someone who can assist the pupil in locating appropriate resources for a project, for example, an adult who can go to the library with the pupil and offer guidance in the process of selecting suitable resources.
* Provide summary sheets of key points from textbooks or lessons that will help pupils digest the information contained in longer pieces of print.
* Provide pupils with reading lists ahead of time, and encourage them to get started with the reading earlier than other pupils who read more quickly.
* Use short or abbreviated reading materials that contain the same intellectual challenge as longer books. For instance, some authors produce short stories as well as novels. Some novels are shorter than others.
* For standardised assessments, such as group tests or public examinations, the pupil's learning difficulties may need to be evaluated and documented before special provisions are made available. For pupils with individual education plans, these provisions will be listed in the IEP.
* Some pupils who have not qualified for special education services may still benefit from modifications and adaptations with tests and examinations. Invite pupils to nominate themselves for modified test or examination conditions (such as extra time) in situations where this is appropriate. For example, when testing a pupil's understanding of a topic in biology, the time taken to demonstrate the required knowledge is immaterial.
* With tests and examinations, it may be appropriate to provide the pupil with a reader. This adult reads the paper to the pupil, without any additional comment. The reader

remains close by throughout the examination and is available to reread sections or clarify particular words if the pupil requires it.

* Some pupils will find it easier to read out loud. If this is the case, allow the pupil to take the exam in a separate room so as not to distract the other pupils.
* Allow extra time for tests and exams. The amount of time allocated will obviously depend on the individual pupil's needs. The length of the test is usually taken into consideration. For example, a pupil may be given an additional ten minutes for each hour of the exam.
* Modify the test so it fits into the time available. In this situation, the pupil is graded on the work they have completed. They are not penalised for the questions that were omitted from the abbreviated test. If they have been given eight questions instead of ten and get all eight correct, then they have scored 100 per cent.
* Some exams start with easy questions with the level of difficulty increasing through the exam paper. Make sure that the pupils have the opportunity to tackle each level of difficulty. It is not appropriate to shorten the paper by removing only the last (difficult) questions. It is better to remove, for example, every fourth question from the entire exam, so the pupil receives questions in all areas, ranging from simple to more advanced questions.

Using technology

* Show the pupils how to use 'AutoSummarize' on their computers. The computer summarises text from sources such as Internet downloads or selected text. Key phrases can be highlighted throughout the text, or an executive summary can be written. The pupil can determine the percentage of reduction. Although not completely accurate, it is a useful tool for the pupils who find it hard to cope with a large volume of print.
* When the class is reading a book, provide an audiotape for the pupil who finds reading difficult. This will help the pupil to keep up with the pace of the reading so they will not be left behind or miss various chapters.
* Have an adult read all or part of the assigned book to help the pupil keep up with classmates.
* Consider using a computer program that uses text to speech for pupils with serious reading difficulties. It reads aloud any text that is selected.

Pupil has difficulties with reading

Reading observation chart: section 3

---

3. Pupil has difficulties with reading

Pupil needs additional time to acquire basic reading skills

Pupil achieves less than other pupils in reading

Pupil needs more support than others when learning how to read

---

Reading is a complex skill involving several different processes, all of which have to be integrated successfully before reading can occur. If you attempt to draw a diagram of the brain circuits involved in reading, you quickly realise that there are many steps between the eye seeing some black lines on the paper and the brain receiving and understanding a meaningful message.

Often pupils are expected to read a previously unseen book in its entirety without any preparation. Let's think about this. Do we expect a musician to pick up a new piece of music and immediately play it completely through? As adults, do we want to read to a congregation in church or at a public meeting without having a chance to preview the reading material? Reading a new book, especially if you have reading difficulties or lack confidence, can be a really daunting challenge.

Given the complexity of the process, it is not surprising that some pupils find it very difficult to learn to read. Maybe the remarkable thing is that so many pupils learn to read quite easily!

> In total, about 15 per cent of pupils have difficulties in learning to read
> About 8 per cent have mild to moderate difficulties
> About 5 per cent have significant difficulties
> About 2 per cent have severe difficulties

Reading is a high-order skill that links language and visual processing.

Developmentally, reading always comes after speech and language have developed. Pupils with severe developmental or language difficulties may never fully master reading.

Pupils with milder, general learning and/or language difficulties will be expected to experience some reading delay in line with their general developmental level. If, for example, a 12-year-old pupil's intellectual or language development is at the level we would usually expect from a 9-year-old, then it is likely that their reading development will also be at around the 9-year-old level. Put another way, if a pupil is in the below average range for intellectual or language skills, then it is likely that reading will also be at a lower than average level.

Some pupils will be disadvantaged by impoverished home circumstances where books are not available and reading is not encouraged. Their early experiences of books and print may be very limited in comparison to many other pupils.

However, many pupils of good (or even exceptional) intelligence, who have excellent support at home and at school, also experience specific reading difficulties.

Reading difficulties are a major barrier to success at school and beyond. To address this disadvantage, two key approaches are required.

Intervention is important. Intervention provides the pupil with appropriate instruction and supported practice over a sufficient period of time. This 'treatment' approach helps to reduce the severity of the reading difficulties, which in turn minimises the disadvantage to the pupil.

Inclusion of pupils with learning difficulties is also vital. Difficulties that would disadvantage the pupil are minimised through a range of adaptations of teaching methods, the curriculum and assessment.

For pupils with reading difficulties, finding a good book to read can be a real problem. Books that are easy enough to read are usually written for younger children. The illustrations and the story line will often be well below the pupil's interest level. On the other hand, books that would be of interest to the pupil are often too difficult for the pupil to read. So it is not surprising that reading is not an enjoyable activity. For many pupils with reading difficulties, the effort of reading just does not seem to be worthwhile.

Strategies for working with reading difficulties

Assessing reading development

* If it has not already been done, arrange for the pupil's reading to be assessed by someone with expertise in the assessment of reading difficulties.
* Use a test that gives both a standardised score and diagnostic information. It is useful to know the exact standard the pupil has reached and to have a clear picture of where difficulties arise. The testing should show you and the pupil where successes have been achieved and indicate where remediation needs to take place.

Providing an effective intervention programme

* Plan an intervention programme (in collaboration with the special education colleagues, if appropriate) that will improve the pupil's skills. Target the pupil's areas of difficulty, and if possible, build on existing strengths.

* Consider using one of the many structured reading programmes available that teach phonetic word decoding in a systematic way. Programmes based on the Orton Gillingham method are well regarded.

* Target the programme based on the pupil's needs. All activities need to be critically evaluated for their instructional value. Is the cutting and pasting making a real contribution to this pupil's learning? ... Is the pupil ready for this reading task?

* Make the programme intensive. Instruction that is repeated or backed up on a daily basis has a much better chance of success than a programme that is only given, say, once a week.

* Combine quality instruction with intensive practice. Many potentially good programmes fail because the pupils are not given enough practice of what has been taught.

* Structure the pupil's programme so that each session is part of a 'stepladder' of learning. Every activity links to previous learning and builds the skills that form the foundation for future learning. Ask yourself, 'What earlier learning is this activity based on? and 'What future learning is this activity leading towards?'

* Pupils forget when they have not consolidated learning well enough. Be sure that one level of skill is firmly established before moving on to the next level.

* Do not rely on reading practice alone to produce gains in reading. Always provide explicit instruction to develop the underlying skills. Reading practice without ongoing instruction may mean that the pupil rehearses inappropriate strategies and fails to develop new, more effective strategies.

* The tasks in your programme will vary in difficulty. Let pupils know if a task is particularly difficult, so they can take pride in their efforts to reach the final goal. Some pupils like to be able to choose their level of difficulty. Offer a choice, and see how some pupils will prefer to opt for a more difficult challenge than you thought. Being able to choose to tackle something difficult can increase motivation. Success with a hard task boosts confidence.

* Teach pupils to learn from their own errors by encouraging them to monitor their own performances and understand their own errors. Ask pupils to devise their own strategies, such as, 'I messed up on that word because I guessed and didn't think about whether it made sense. Next time I'll think about what it means.'

* Set explicit, achievable reading goals. Break the pupil's reading programme into small, achievable sections. Make each learning goal explicit, and describe how it will be assessed. Vague goals, such as 'Bart will improve his reading', make the task seem endless. Bart and his teachers won't have any way of knowing whether or not they are achieving the goal.

  Table 2.1 provides an example of writing a specific goal for a pupil, setting a time limit and describing a plan for assessing the pupil's progress towards achievement of the goal.

* Show the pupil how much they are learning, not how much there is to learn. Create a chart so that both you and the pupil can see that progress is being made. You could use Appendix Form 33: 'Pupil guide to setting goals' or Appendix Form 23: 'Teacher checklist for mastery learning'.

* Reward cooperation with reading practice. For younger pupils, create a chart that records the amount of time spent reading. You can use Appendix Form 8: '100 minutes reading' chart, or make your own. Create a chart with 100 squares. Each square represents one minute of reading. If the pupil reads for four minutes, the pupil will

Table 2.1 Writing pupil goals

Specify what the pupil will achieve.	Bart will be able to read 50 of the most commonly used words.
Set a time limit.	Bart will be able to read these words by the end of the term.
Describe your assessment plan.	We will write all 50 words on note cards. Each time Bart reads a word correctly, we will place a star on the back of the card. When a card has 5 stars Bart will have finished with that word. He can tear the card up and throw it away.

colour or stamp four squares. Give small rewards for reading a total of 10 minutes and a larger reward for reading for 100 minutes.

✷ For older pupils, negotiate a reward system in return for compliance with the reading programme. Rewards which are meaningful to the pupil work best. So ask the pupil to select rewards from a predetermined list, which the pupil can add to if desired. Use Appendix Form 33: 'Pupil guide to setting goals' for this.

✷ Add an extra incentive for good attitude. For example, the pupil might be paid £1 for completing the reading task and £2 for completing the task without complaining or wasting time. This, of course, needs to be arranged with the parent in advance. Appendix Form 33: 'Pupil guide to setting goals' provides a section for this.

✷ Make sure definite time limits are set for how long the pupil has to work on reading skills. Some pupils feel overwhelmed thinking that the reading session is going to go on 'forever'. Knowing that there is a definite time limit helps the pupil to settle down and get through the required work in the allotted time.

✷ Celebrate the achievement of learning goals. Negotiate with the pupil the type of achievement celebration they would like. Perhaps the pupil simply would like a certificate to take home to show parents and grandparents, or possibly a special treat or privilege during the school day.

✷ Select reading materials that suit the pupil's reading ability and age/image.

✷ It is particularly important to make sure the books chosen are of interest to the pupil. So check with the pupil to make sure the books have intrinsic interest.

✷ Locate publishers that produce books especially for older readers with reading difficulties and make these available. Enlist the help of the librarian or media specialist to find books that will suit the pupil.

✷ Read interesting and exciting articles and books to the pupils. This helps pupils to see that reading is interesting and is definitely a skill worth acquiring.

✷ Create a personal reading folder with the pupil. Select magazine and newspaper reports that interest the pupil. Photocopy and enlarge the articles and paste the articles into the folder. The pupil may have special interest in a favourite sports team or movie star and could accumulate articles of interest throughout the year.

✷ Create a group or class folder on a topic of shared interest, and encourage all pupils to look at home for articles that can be brought to school and placed in the reading folder.

✷ Choose an appropriate time for interventions. If possible, arrange it so the extra help occurs at a time that does not unsettle the pupil. Missing out on recreation, a favourite subject or an opportunity to have fun is a sure way to make the pupil feel negative about a reading programme.

✷ For younger pupils or pupils who have major reading difficulties, look at the time of day that suits them best. The pupil with difficulties in learning may be very tired by the afternoon and may learn best earlier in the day.

✷ Keep a careful register of books that the pupil has read so you will know if the pupil is returning to the same book time and time again. You will also be able to monitor the difficulty level that the pupil is selecting.

* Remember to teach, not test. Teaching involves providing pupils with tasks that are at the margin of their competence. The books should not be so easy that the pupils feel bored or 'put down', nor so hard that the pupils feel overwhelmed and anxious. The teacher should work in partnership with the pupils, providing as much help, support and coaching as needed to enable each to succeed with the task.

* If a pupil needs an excessive amount of help, then the task itself is too difficult. If the pupil needs little or no help, then the task set is too easy for new learning to occur. Easy tasks do have their place in consolidating skills and building confidence.

* If the pupil becomes mixed up or confused when reading a particular section, quickly and quietly join in to help them through the difficult part, and then fade out once the pupil is reading smoothly again.

* Try to avoid giving complex instruction in the middle of a pupil's reading. Allow the pupil to continue reading (with your help if needed), and then revisit the difficult sections once the reading has been completed.

* Some pupils get very flustered reading out loud. Clarify what they should do if they encounter a word they don't know. Some pupils like to be allowed some time to try to work the word out for themselves, with a prearranged signal (such as tapping on the table), if they need the adult to help.

* If the pupil selects a book that's challenging, read the entire book in tandem with the pupil. With both adult and pupil reading along together, the pupil takes the lead for most of the time. The adult takes the lead when the pupil encounters a difficult section. It can take a little while to develop the skill of reading in tandem, but once established, this method is a good way to help an anxious pupil read with fluency and confidence. It also helps to provide the pupil with access to books that they could not read unaided.

* Move from the familiar to the new in small steps. Provide a structured set of reading books that are very carefully graded for difficulty. Introduce a slightly harder book to the pupil and show the pupil where the new challenges are. Help the pupil to tackle these new challenges by explicit teaching and support. 'See, this book is almost the same as your favourite. Let's see now. Here are a few new words. Let's learn them first so you can go right ahead and read the new book by yourself.'

* Take a book and, with the pupil, rewrite it, adding more detail and dialogue than the original, using the pupil's own words. Print out the new and expanded version of the story, and have the pupil read the revised edition.

* Ask the pupil to dictate their own reading materials. First, the pupil tells the story and the adult types it. Then the story is printed and forms a new book for the pupil to read.

* Encourage rehearsal (or rereading) for improved confidence and skill. Introduce reading materials that have to be rehearsed, such as a speech to be given to the class or an acting part in a play. The pupils can rehearse (and reread) as often as necessary until they feel ready to 'perform'.

* Some pupils are happy to read a 'little kid's' book, if it's for a genuine purpose. Check to see if your older pupil would like to read a play or a story to a group of younger pupils.

* Build a library of story tapes for the younger pupils in your school by having older pupils (who need the reading practice) create the tapes by using rehearsed reading. The pupils can add expression and sound effects and make up different voices for characters to add interest to the recording.

Pupil does not understand how reading 'works'

Reading observation chart: section 4

---

4. Pupil does not understand how reading 'works'

Pupil thinks that reading happens automatically

Pupil does not realise that skilled readers have to work hard at times

Pupil does not think about own reading strategies

It can be difficult for pupils with reading problems to see the complete picture of what they are learning and how they are progressing. We know that *metacognition* (thinking about your own thinking) can be a very useful tool in learning.

Pupils progress more quickly if they understand what strategies they are already using successfully and which skills they need to work on. Many pupils with reading difficulties downgrade their own skills, because they misunderstand how good readers perform. They assume that good readers:

- always know every word right away without sounding out or guessing
- always understand something the first time they read it
- never need to read anything more than once
- can always read fluently and expressively
- can read any book in a very short period of time
- have total recall of every word they have read.

Paul, who was 13 and struggling with reading, explained: 'The other kids, they read a book and it's like they've just seen the movie. They just sit there, and then they've finished the book.'

Frank, a successful businessman but poor reader, said, 'I'd like to be able to do like the teachers do – go to a library and read all the books and know everything about everything in that library. Me? I pick up a book and read the first chapter, but I couldn't even tell you everything in that chapter.'

If poor readers believe that others can read a book in the same time it takes to watch the movie, or that people who can read transfer the contents of a library into their own minds, then it's not surprising they feel inadequate and frustrated by their own reading skills.

Strategies for helping pupils understand the reading process

Talking about reading

✱ Have a class discussion about reading strategies that pupils who are good readers implement. It is helpful for pupils who are struggling with reading to understand that all readers, even those who appear skilled, do have to work at the process, and that strategies such as the following are a normal part of skilled reading.
  - sounding out unfamiliar words
  - using the context to guess at a word
  - reading something through several times
  - making notes on important points
  - using the index or chapter headings to select what is most important

- • skimming the text when searching for information
- • asking for clarification from others
- • taking many hours to read through a lengthy book
* Before a pupil starts to read to you, ask the pupil what strategies might be needed.
  - • 'Does this book look like you can read it through just once?'
  - • 'It looks as if there might be some hard words in this book. What will you do if you come across a word you are not sure of?'
  - • 'This is a big book, and you only want to find out about penguins, so what is the best plan?'
* Ask the pupil to describe the strategies they are using. Discuss what other tactics they might be able to use.
  - • 'I was guessing because I knew the story. I could try sounding out the words.'
  - • 'That took too long. I should have used the index to find the information I needed.'
* Ask the pupils to listen to self-made tape recordings of themselves reading. What do they notice about how they read? Are they too hesitant? What could they do to fix this problem? Did they stumble on hard words? What could they do about that?

Pupil has difficulties with phonics

Reading observation chart: section 5

---

5. Pupil has difficulties with phonics

Pupil has difficulties remembering letter shapes

Pupil makes errors when sounding out single letters

Pupil makes errors when sounding out letter blends

The ability to use phonics is a critical foundation skill in reading. The ability to sound out words allows the pupil to move beyond reading whole words by sight. Once phonic skills are firmly established, the pupil can become an independent learner. They can read new and unfamiliar words without assistance and steadily build the repertoire of words they can read with ease.

Even as adults, we use phonics to continue to extend our reading. When we encounter new words, such as *unchup* or *hinbeek*, we put our existing knowledge of letter patterns and their sounds into action and read the word. The process is quick and inconspicuous, because we are so skilled at it.

Pupils also have to be able to learn the connection between a sound and a letter shape. Even if they can recognise the *d* sound in *dog*, they still have to be able to remember that the sound only matches the *d* letter, and that similar looking letters, such as *b* and *p*, have their own sounds.

Quite a few letters can be easily confused with each other. Letters such as *b* and *d* may be reversed, or letters such as *u* and *n* may be inverted. Pupils also have to learn that every letter has an uppercase and a lowercase form and that sometimes the lowercase is just a miniature of the uppercase, but sometimes it is not!

The pupils also have to be able to detect quite subtle differences between sounds. For example, say the sounds *c* and *g* to yourself and notice how similar these sounds are to one another.

Some pupils also get mixed up between letter sounds and letter names. Many children's books and computer programs use letter names and uppercase letters for preschool learning. Parents may also use letter names and teach capitals for the child's first reading and writing experiences.

Our alphabet is confusing. Every letter has a name and at least one sound. Some letters change sound depending on their position in a word and some letters make a new sound when they are combined with one or more other letters. Some letters have a name that starts with their own sound, some do not!

Go through the alphabet for yourself now, and see which letter names actually start with their own sound. For example:

* Name the letter *W*. This letter's name starts with the *d* sound!
* Name the letter *B*. This letter's name starts with the *b* sound!
* Name the letter *Y*. This letter's name starts with the *w* sound!

Confusing isn't it?

Many pupils with learning difficulties will not have completely mastered the phonic system when it was being taught in the general classroom. They may have learned enough to get by, and may have become skillful in bluffing their way through. However, these pupils tend to slip through the cracks once explicit instruction and overt practice have finished. We know that one of the hallmarks of a reading disorder is a slow response to appropriate intervention. Many of these pupils will have only a fragile hold on phonics and will need the skills to be regularly taught, practised and revised over an extended period.

Strategies for teaching phonics: letters and sounds

Establishing the basics

* Teach the basics of letter names and sounds. Ensure that the pupil understands the difference between a letter name and a letter sound.
* Teach the upper- and lowercase form of each letter. Teach when capital letters are used.
* Encourage parents to use lowercase letters when teaching the alphabet to their children.
* For some pupils, this learning will need to be carefully structured and taken at a slow pace to make sure that each letter being taught is thoroughly known before the next one is introduced.
* Check that the pupil is able to give the sounds for all single letters before you expect them to be able to read using basic phonics. Appendix Form 6: 'Diagnostic phonics assessment' will help you to do this.
* Teach contrasting letters and sounds first to avoid confusion. It is easier to learn contrasting letter shapes and sounds such as *o* and *f* rather than letters that sound and look quite similar to each other, such as *t* and *f*.
* Teach parents the basics of phonics, so they understand and support what you are doing in school. Help parents to select early learning materials that provide practice in letter sounds and lowercase letters.
* Provide parents with suitable resources that they can refer to if they are not sure of letter sounds themselves – for instance, a chart that gives a letter and a word that prompts its sound: *a* as in *cat*, *d* as in *dog*, etc.
* Be prepared to teach and revise the same basics over and over again to pupils with reading difficulties.
* Check that older pupils still retain the basics, as often they will use letter names instead of sounds if they are not carefully monitored.

✳   Some pupils believe that sounding out is only for little kids. Reassure the pupils that adults often use sounding out too. It is one of the most important ways of reading new words, however old we are.

Pupil has difficulties with phonological awareness and word building

Reading observation chart: section 6

---

6. Pupil has difficulties with phonological awareness and word building

Pupil makes errors when trying to hear sounds in words

Pupil makes errors when blending sounds together

Pupil makes errors reading new words. (See Appendix Form 6: 'Diagnostic phonics assessment'.)

Many pupils with reading difficulties find phonics difficult at first. The pupil needs good phonological awareness (the ability to recognise segments of speech within words) before early instruction in letters and their sounds make much sense to them.

If you can't hear that *man* is made up of the sounds *m-a-n*, then being told that the letter *m* makes the special *mmm* sound doesn't make much sense. Things that don't make much sense are hard to remember and put into action.

Once the pupil does know all the letter sounds, they have to be able to blend those sounds together and make recognisable words. Again, this can be a real stumbling block for some pupils. The pupil will produce a string of sounds such as *t-w-i-s-t* but think that the word is *whistle* or *twin*, or even invent a word, such as *tittles*. These difficulties show us that the pupil has difficulty with the phonological skill of hearing the link between *t-w-i-s-t* and the word *twist*.

In most schools, phonics are thoroughly taught in the early years. Children with good phonological skills usually pick up the idea quickly and are soon successfully using letter sounds to work out words.

Strategies for developing phonological awareness and word building skills

Working with auditory discrimination

✳   If the pupil seems to have a lot of difficulty with discriminating the subtle differences between sounds, ask the parents to arrange for a hearing test. Some children (especially those with a history of recurrent middle ear infections) may have problems with auditory discrimination.

✳   Relate sounds to real words. When using prompts, such as '*s* is for *sun*', always give several examples. This helps the pupil to understand that the letter *s* and its sound occur in many words, not just *sun*. For example, teach '*s* is for *sun, sand, sit…*'.

✳   Encourage pupils to think of their own words for sounds. If a pupil has trouble doing this, it's a warning sign that the pupil has difficulties with phonological skills.

✳   Some pupils will need additional prompts. You could put out some objects (or pictures) on the desk, such as a cup, pen, box, tin, hat, sock, and pin, and sound out the names. The pupil has to listen and say which item you are sounding out. For example, you sound out *p-i-n*, and the pupil points to the pin and says 'pin'.

Linking listening with written words

✳   Teach letters in groups that can be put into words, so the pupils see the point of the learning and understand how to put their newfound knowledge into action. Teach all

Table 2.2 Stages of phonics instruction

Stage 1	Use words in the consonant–vowel–consonant pattern. For example: *set, pet, wet* or *pin, win, tin, bin* or *fat, cat, hat*. Notice that often these words can be clustered in groups that share the same vowel-consonant ending (called the rime) but have different initial letters (called the onset). Teaching onset–rime patterns makes this first stage much easier, because the learning from one word can be generalised to the next. If you can read *pin*, it is easy to read *win, bin* and *tin*.
Stage 2	Two consonants sliding together. For example *trip, spin, stop* Two consonants making a new sound. For example *ship, chop, thin* Final *e*. For example *hope, take, like* Use a maximum of four letters in each word, so the pupil only has to deal with one letter blend.
Stage 3	Two vowels making a new sound. For example *out, feet, boat* Vowel and consonant making a new sound. For example *part, dawn, dirt* Silent letters. For example *gnaw, knot*
Stage 4	Three consonants sliding together. For example *shrug, strap, scream* Four letters making a new sound. For example *ration, light, rough* Words ending in *y* or *ing*. For example *happy, silly, tapping, ring*
Stage 5	Words that combine two or more of the previously taught patterns. For example *combine, sprout, market* Words that are compound words; words using prefixes or suffixes. For example *preview, unhappy, defeat*

the letters in words such as *sun*, *bat* and *pig*. Then show the pupils how they can mix and match the letters they know and read words such as *sun, bun, gun, bat, pat, nut, bit* ... .

* Teach blending skills once you are sure that the pupil can confidently give the correct sound for each letter. Some pupils find it hard to blend sounds together to make whole words. If this is a problem, then give them practice in listening to strings of sounds that you produce and guessing at the word you are reading. For instance, you read *c-u-p*, and the pupil says 'cup'. This is an easier task then having to sound and blend for themselves.

* Build phonological skills in graduated steps. Choose a reading programme that has a phonic basis, so the reading materials provided will reinforce phonic skills. Books written in rhyme (such as the Dr Seuss books) are often very good sources of phonic reading and can be lots of fun, too.

* Give pupils short, simple words that only contain one challenge. For instance, if you are teaching words with the blend *sh*, stay with short words, so that apart from the *sh*, all the other letters have single sounds. Good words would include *shop, ship, dish*. On the other hand, teaching *sh* in words such as *shopping, shoe, pushing* makes the word itself too hard. The pupils have several different phonic challenges to handle at the same time. This distracts them from the *sh* blend that they are trying to learn.

* Try to keep what you teach clear and carefully structured. Deal with the levels of difficulty systematically, so your pupils build skills and confidence by moving from easier phonic tasks to more difficult ones. Refer to the following chart for examples.

* Use magnetic letters or letter cards (lowercase) to encourage pupils to play with word building and reading. Start with building three-letter words, and colour code the vowels. Teach that these colour-coded letters should be placed in the middle of the word for this early word building game.

* Teach the pupils to recognise vowels and consonants.

* Use reading analogies to show pupils how to use known words to read unknown ones. Write pairs of words that share the same pattern. Read the first word to the pupil and ask the pupil to work out the second word in the pair. 'If this word says "seed", what does this word [need] say? ... How do you know that?' Encourage the pupil to

'shortcut' sounding out by recognising that by substituting one letter of a word with another, they can read a new word very easily.

* Ask the pupil to change a word one letter at a time and see how many words they can make. For example, they may begin with the word *give* and then change the word, one letter at a time: *live, line, lane, pane, pine, pink, wink*, etc.

* Provide the pupil an ample selection of letters, syllables and small words written on cards. The pupil can create both real and nonsense words by putting cards end to end and then reading the newly created words. This really helps to create confidence and can be lots of fun.

* Provide the pupil with multi-syllable words written on cards, and ask the pupil to cut the words up into syllables, prefixes and suffixes. Ask the pupil to use these word segments to make other words. The pupil can choose to use the segments he already has or write any new ones that are needed. For example, a pupil may take the word *caravan* and cut it up into three segments: *car a van*. They can then take *car* and turn it into *scar, carry, carwash* by adding new letters and words.

Pupil has difficulties recognising words at sight

Reading observation chart: section 7

---

7. Pupil has difficulties recognising words at sight

Pupil makes errors when attempting to read everyday words

Pupil can read words in a familiar book but cannot read the same words out of context

Pupil relies on pictures to get sense of story

Pupil makes many errors and self-corrections when reading

Pupil confuses words of similar appearance, such as *bread* and *bird*

Pupil makes errors when copying words

Pupil reads word by word

Pupil puts in different words but keeps the meaning of the story. For example, reads *Jane got a present for her birthday* instead of *Jane got a parcel for her birthday.*

All pupils need to be able to read using phonics (sounding out letters and blending the sounds together). However, pupils also need to be able to recognise words at sight. In English, some words are irregular and simply do not sound out. Other words occur so frequently that sounding out over and over again is just not practical.

Many pupils with reading difficulties have problems in remembering the appearance of commonly used words, such as *the, they, my, am, are, is, here* and *where*. Even though the pupil may see these words literally hundreds of times, they may still 'forget' them over and over again. Adults can get very frustrated when pupils constantly forget these apparently easy words.

However, we need to remember that print is easiest to recall if it has an unusual visual pattern and conjures up a picture or feeling for reader. Words such as *spaghetti, elephant,* and *tyrannosaurus rex* have quite distinctive patterns and grab the young reader's interest. On the other hand, words such as *the, they, my, am, are, is, here* and *where* have no distinctive visual pattern and are often easily confused with one another. Some pupils find it very hard to remember these frustrating little words through exposure in everyday reading. For them, a more explicit and deliberate teaching approach needs to be used.

Accurate reading depends on the ability to make distinctions between words that look quite similar such as *beard* and *bread, trail* and *trial* or *king* and *knight*. Pupils who find this difficult often rely heavily on the context of the story, using a mixture of 'look and guess' and picking up some clues from the sounds of the letters. However, they may overlook the sequence of the letters or rely too heavily on context.

Traditional readers often had 'controlled' vocabulary. This meant that new words were introduced gradually and each new word was repeated several times over. The reading books were often in a numbered sequence, so the pupil moved through the levels of difficulty in a gradual way. The downside was that the readers were often repetitive and uninteresting. These readers are now rather out of fashion, but they still have their place, particularly for pupils with learning difficulties.

Pupils who have difficulty remembering the appearance of words often have trouble copying accurately. They may copy letter by letter because they are unable to remember whole words or phrases, or because the words they are writing are meaningless to them.

Looking at a printed word and saying that word automatically is quite a high-order skill. Fortunately, there is a ladder of easier tasks that can be introduced first to build up a pupil's ability to recognise key words by sight.

Strategies for developing word recognition skills

Using a hierarchy of learning

✴ Check that the pupil can read commonly used words automatically. Use Appendix Form 5: '100 most frequently used words' to do this.

✴ Use a graded sequence of activities to develop word recognition. Select about 15 to 20 words that you are going to teach. For pupils who are struggling, it is a good idea to select some words that are high interest and visually distinctive. You could use names of the pupils' friends or families, favorite foods or animals. Reading a long and interesting word such as *tyrannosaurus* is much more exciting and confidence building than being able to read *when*. The pupil will never guess that the long word is actually much easier to recognise by sight! (See Table 2.3.)

Table 2.3 Hierarchy of teaching strategies for whole words

Match to sample when the sample is in view	At this stage, the pupil is asked only to match the target word to an identical sample. The sample remains in view the entire time as the pupil searches for words that match. Keep one card as a sample. Place the word in the pupil's view. Ask the pupil to sort the other cards into groups to match the sample. 'Look … this word is *went*. See if you can find all the other cards that say *went*. Check with the sample if you are not sure. I'll leave it right here for you to see.' You can repeat the process with all the words you are teaching.
Match to sample when the sample is hidden	This is the same as the previous step, except that once the pupil has been shown the sample word, it is hidden from view. 'This card says *went*. Have a good look before I turn it over. Do you think you can remember it? Okay, I'm turning it over so you can't peek. Now see if you can find all the other cards that have *went* on them."
Recognition	Working with the same cards as before, the pupil is now required to recognise the words on the cards but does not have a sample to match. The cards are spread out, and this time the pupil is asked, 'Can you find me the word that says *went*?' If the pupil is confused, allow the pupil to look at the sample card before it is hidden again.
Reading	At this stage, the pupil is reading the words without any prompts. Point to individual words and ask, 'What is this word?' Work through all the words you have been teaching, presenting them in jumbled order. If the pupil is confused by this, then show four cards that all have the same word on them, one after the other. When the pupil becomes more confident, go back to presenting the word cards in jumbled order.
Consolidation	Stack all the words that have been taught into a pack. Shuffle the cards and deal them. Increase the speed as you go, until the pupil can read each word quickly as it appears. Games such as 'Word Snap' and 'Word Lotto' can provide additional practice, if necessary.

✳ Take just four or five words from your list to work on at any one time, gradually building up the word list as the pupil progresses. Write all of the words on separate cards. Make several sets of each word.

✳ Use real sentences to practise word recognition with an activity called transformations. This can easily be combined with the activity described above and is a very effective way of teaching whole word recognition skills. In this activity, the pupil learns to recognise whole words in a real language context. (See Table 2.4.)

✳ Make activities and games where reading words and phrases is all part of a game.

Making learning fun

✳ Create a treasure hunt! Write simple clues (at the pupil's level), which if read correctly, will lead to a prize. 'Look under the teacher's table…. Go to the back of the classroom…. Open the blue cupboard.' It's a good idea to read the options to the pupils first, so that when they play the game, they already know the range of words they are likely to encounter.

✳ Write the names of various edible and non-edible items on strips of paper. Put all the strips into a box, and have pupils take a 'lucky dip' into the box to select one of the items listed. For example, pupils may create their own special pizza topping. Perhaps the pupil will end up with a *banana*, *ham*, *cheese* and *old sock* pizza!

✳ Ask pupils to select their outfits for the day by taking a lucky dip from a variety of clothing items. Maybe they will end up with *jeans, a wedding dress* and *a space helmet*!

✳ Write characters and their actions on slips of paper, and play charades. The pupil chooses a paper, reads the scenario and acts the out the part for the others to guess: e.g., *a horse jumping; a cook making a cake;* or *a dog hiding a bone.*

✳ Write names of popular heroes, family, friends and fictitious characters, and take a lucky dip to find out the guests to your next birthday: e.g., *Batman, Mum, a green jelly monster, Mrs Nichols* and *a duck.*

✳ Encourage your pupils to use written language to communicate. Exchanging letters with pupils in other schools via the Internet or postal service is a great way to develop an interest in the written word.

Table 2.4 Transformations: reading words as real language

Say a sentence	Work with the pupil to produce a sentence. If possible, the sentence should be the pupil's own, although sometimes a combined effort works better.
Write the sentence	Write the sentence clearly on a strip of paper or card. Read the sentence back with the pupil, so the pupil understands that the language is now in print form. Keep a copy of the sentence if you think the pupil will need a sample to work from when they build the sentence up from individual words.
Cut the sentence	With the pupil's help, cut the sentence into parts. Generally, cut each word apart from the sentence. Sometimes you might choose to keep a phrase such as "Once upon a time" together on a single strip of paper.
Scramble the words	Scramble the words and phrases.
Rebuild the sentence	Have the pupil reassemble the sentence in its original order. If the pupil finds this difficult, provide a sample sentence to work from, so the pupil can match the words one by one.
Make a new sentence	Work with the pupil to see how the words in the sentence can be rearranged, and perhaps how new words can be added.
Save the sentence	Have the pupil paste the sentence into a blank book made for this purpose as a reading resource the pupil can read again another day.

✳ Use a classroom bulletin board as a communication spot where pupils can post information to be read by other pupils. Jokes, amazing facts, cartoons, announcements of school and community events, invitations to sign up for recess sports, etc. can all entice reluctant readers to read for information.

Providing repetition and consolidation

✳ Make sure that there is enough repetition of hard-to-remember whole words to develop solid learning.

✳ Provide reading materials with a high level of 'scaffolding', or support. For instance, create a set of questions. The question is read out loud by the adult, and the pupil reads the answer. The question and the answer contain many of the same words, so the pupil has a very strong framework to rely on. For example:

　　Question:　Which animal *likes to catch mice?*
　　Answer:　　The cat *likes to catch mice.*

✳ Some pupils who read a book once simply read and forget the new words over and over again. These pupils need activities where the reading vocabulary in one book is taught and reinforced in a variety of ways.

✳ Introduce a new reading book by doing some preparatory work, even before the book is opened. Teach new words that will be encountered, revise words that have proven difficult in earlier books and introduce the topic and related vocabulary.

✳ The book can be used in a variety of ways. Of course the pupil will read the book, possibly several times. The words that present difficulty can be singled out for additional practice.

✳ The pupil may create additional books that have the same reading vocabulary as the original. These books can provide additional practice with reading the difficult words along with the rest of the vocabulary.

✳ Word games, such as 'Word Lotto', 'Word Pairs' and 'Word Snap', are sentence-building activities that can reinforce new words. These games can easily be created to use in the classroom. There are many variations for these three games.

　　'Word Lotto': The teacher prepares four playing boards so that four players can participate. Each board is marked off as a grid. The teacher selects 24 words that are being taught and writes six of these words on each board. Any sections of the board that do not contain a word can be coloured in. The teacher then writes the same 24 words on 24 small cards to fit the dimensions of the playing board. These small cards are shuffled and shown to the pupils one-by-one. If the card shown matches a word on a pupil's card, then that pupil can claim the card. The pupil must be able to read the word before they can claim it. The pupil places the card on top of the word on the board. The pupil who fills their board first is the winner.

　　'Word Pairs': Use index cards to create pairs of words. The word cards are mixed up and placed face down on the table. The pupils take turns turning over cards to see if they can get two matching words. Spelling words, vocabulary words or any reinforcement words may be used. For a more difficult version, pupils must be able to define the word before winning the pair.

　　'Word Snap': Select 10 words, and make four to six copies of each of the words (40–60 cards in all). The cards are shuffled and placed in the centre of the table. Each player draws a card from the centre pile and places the card face up in the discard pile. When the same word appears twice in a row, the players shout "Snap!" The first player to shout "Snap!" wins the pair of words. The player with the largest number of pairs wins the game.

✳ Pupils should not begin a new book until they have mastered at least 95 per cent of all the words in their present reader. If this takes too long to achieve, the book is too hard and the pupils will become too frustrated. A substitute book should be chosen or supplementary reading activities given to teach the words in the book.

* Provide challenges in word discrimination. The pupils have to select one word from a pair of words that look quite similar. For example, the pupil may be asked to listen to a sentence that is read out loud and then underline the correct words: e.g., 'When Jack came home, he found a *parcel/packet* by the *room/door*.' Or, 'As the *king/knight* rode into view, the crowds all rushed to *greet/great* him.'
* Preview or pre-read the book to the pupil to prepare them for the unfamiliar words.
* Provide an audiotape of the book, so the pupil can read along with the tape.
* Support the pupil who is slow to read and copy words. Provide a printed copy of the notes, and ensure that the pupil understands what is written. Either read the paper to the pupil, or support the pupil as they read it through.

Pupil has difficulties with reading fluency

Reading observation chart: section 8

8. Pupil has difficulties with reading fluency

Pupil's oral language is hesitant and lacks fluency

Pupil stammers when speaking and reading

Pupil cannot find the right word when reading

Pupil's reading is hesitant and stilted

Pupil takes a long time to recognise words

Pupil sounds out the same words over and over again

Pupil does not use punctuation to guide reading

Pupil reads so slowly that the amount of practice is limited

Some pupils have general difficulties with fluent speech, and this can have an impact on their ordinary speaking and on their reading. They may stammer or have difficulties producing a fluent sequence of words when talking and when reading aloud.

However, many verbal fluency problems are caused by 'word finding' difficulties. When the pupil attempts to answer a question in class, they may get stuck halfway through because they are unable to 'find' the right word. When the pupil is reading, the same thing happens. They see the word but cannot name it quickly enough, even though it is recognised. as familiar. In this situation, reading may be slow and disjointed because of general language production problems rather than a reading difficulty.

Pupils may also be self-conscious and nervous about reading out loud, and this, too, can have a direct impact on their fluency and expression. In particular, pupils may feel embarrassed to read with expression, fearing that they may sound silly if they read in an exaggerated or dramatic manner.

For some, early reading difficulties may have created the habit of reading word-by-word without expression. Sometimes, even when reading skills have improved considerably, the old habit of slow and disjointed reading continues.

Other pupils' reading may lack expression because they are not following the story line well enough to pick up the meaning. Perhaps they are working so hard to work out individual words that they lose sight of the sentence, or perhaps they experience general difficulties with the comprehension of language.

Punctuation can make all the difference to the fluency of what is read. Punctuation gives shape and structure to the text and sometimes even alters meaning. For the pupil who finds getting through the words more than enough of a challenge, punctuation is often ignored. This can lead to poorer comprehension of the text, which in turn, results in limited expression and fluency.

Lack of 'automaticity' (the ability to recognise a word at sight) in reading is a very common characteristic of pupils with poor fluency. The pupil either has to study the word carefully and hope that they can retrieve its name, or they have to sound out the word to decode it using phonics. Both processes are slow and make the reading sound disjointed.

If a pupil reads word by word, then the process will be tedious and less enjoyable. The pupil will also be more likely to miss out on the necessary quantity of practice that is essential for the development of reading skills.

Although explicit teaching is very important in the development of good reading skills, the old saying 'Practice makes perfect' certainly also applies. For the pupil who reads very slowly, the amount of practice the pupil experiences may be significantly reduced in comparison with more skilled and speedy readers. This means that the pupil is doubly disadvantaged by poor reading skills combined with lack of practice.

Strategies for developing reading fluency

Understanding why the pupil lacks fluency

* Assess the pupil's reading through silent reading tests.
  * Is the pupil able to read more quickly when reading silently?
  * Can the pupil do better with reading comprehension if reading silently?
  * Can the pupil accurately fill in missing words in the text if reading silently?
    If the answer to these questions is yes, then the pupil does not actually have a reading problem – only a difficulty with the verbal fluency needed for oral reading. If the pupil has poor oral fluency, allow the pupil to read silently rather than out loud.
* A speech pathologist will be able to give advice for improving oral fluency.
* Improving fluency.
* If it is essential for the pupil to read out loud, allow the pupil time for additional practice.
* Rehearse fluent reading by reading in unison with the pupil. Read along with the pupil, setting the pace somewhat faster than the pupil's own natural speed, so that as they read with you, they are forced to read a little more quickly. Then ask the pupil to read unaided, and encourage them to keep up the pace of the reading that was practised together.
* Move a marker under the words slightly faster than the pupil's natural speed. Encourage the pupil to keep pace with the marker.
* Have the pupil move the marker, and encourage the pupil to read as smoothly and quickly as they are able. Ask the pupil to read along with an audiotape that sets a reasonable pace to help develop verbal fluency when reading.
* Offer the pupil options for audience and setting. Some pupils much prefer to read at home, some will read willingly to a supportive older pupil, and others may prefer one-to-one with a teacher or other adult.
* Show that fluent, expressive reading is a good thing to be able to do. Role models with fluent and expressive reading are very valuable. An adult, older pupil or classmate reading an exciting book with expression and fluency to the class can make a real difference to your pupils' understanding that it is acceptable to read with enthusiasm.
* Encourage theatrical reading, where the dialogue of the script encourages the readers to take on the personality of the characters and read with expression. Reading a script also allows for rehearsal, which is important in developing reading skills.
* Have pupils read and reread a passage until they are fluent, accurate and confident. Use a stopwatch to encourage pupils to speed up and decrease the amount of time it takes to read the passage. This helps to build 'automaticity'.
* Some pupils have a habit of sounding out words that they know perfectly well. Give the pupil rapid word reading practice with flash cards to change this habit.

* Run your finger or a pencil underneath the print as the pupil reads to encourage smooth, speedy reading. Encourage the pupil to do the same when he reading silently.
* Make sure the pupils practise their reading daily, for at least 20 minutes, to build their skills. Nobody is fluent at a skill that is never practised.
* Highlight phrases to show the pupil which words should be read together in one breath: *Once upon a time / there was a wicked witch / called Bernadette.*
* Check the difficulty level of the book to be sure that the pupil can read it with a reasonable degree of fluency. If the book is too difficult for the pupil, reading will inevitably be slow and frustrating. The pupil should be able to read at least nine out of every ten words to be able to read with understanding and fluency.
* Teach the pupil to use punctuation to aid fluent, expressive reading. Ask the pupils to go through the selected reading before beginning to read. Use a brightly coloured highlighter to mark the punctuation marks. Discuss what the punctuation marks mean and how they are used during reading, and then encourage the pupil to apply these skills while reading.
* Provide your pupils with printed text where all the punctuation has been removed. Read the text to the pupils, emphasising the pauses and expression. Ask the pupils to fill in the punctuation marks as you read.

Pupil has difficulties making sense of what is read

Reading observation chart: section 9

---
9. Pupil has difficulties making sense of what is read

Pupil puts in words that do not make sense. For example: *Jane got a playing for her birthday.*

Pupil makes up words. For example: *Jane got a purrel for her birthday.*

Pupil makes errors answering reading comprehension questions

Unfortunately for many pupils with reading difficulties, understanding the story is the last thing on their minds! They have such a struggle working out the words, that they are only too pleased to be able to stop as soon as the final word is reached.

Pupils may rely on working out and guessing words one by one. They insert nonsense words, or words that do not make sense, when they come to an unknown word. Being able to understand, remember *and* discuss the meaning of what has been read can be very challenging indeed.

There is an unusual group of pupils whose reading accuracy and speed are phenomenal, but whose reading comprehension is poor. While not many pupils fall into this group, it is important to be aware that such a pattern is possible. This phenomena is called 'hyperlexia'.

Some pupils with general language difficulties will also have reading difficulties. Strictly speaking, they may not have a reading problem as such, rather they may have limitation in the way they understand language, whether it is spoken or written. However, such language difficulties are often most clearly apparent in the pupil's reading. Typically, they may find it hard to maintain the correct grammar of the sentences and superimpose their own, rather disordered, grammar in place of what is written on the page.

Some pupils with reading difficulties do manage to grasp the factual information they have read, but they fail to move on to make deductions, inferences and predictions.

It is often difficult for pupils with learning difficulties to formulate an answer in comprehension. They do not always understand that reading comprehension is quite different from the informal question-and-answer exchanges that occur in conversation. In conversation, it is fine to say 'yes', but in written language, an expanded response is required.

Strategies for making sense of reading

Finding the right level of difficulty for the pupil

* No pupil will understand reading material that is too difficult for them to read. So make sure that the pupil can read the story reasonably accurately and fluently.
* The language and ideas in the book must also be at an appropriate level to suit the pupil's own level of language and cognitive development.
* You may need to ask for a psychologist or speech pathologist to assess the pupil's general language or cognitive abilities, if the pupil experiences major difficulties with reading comprehension.

Highlighting meaning

* Prepare some reading passages with every ninth word deleted. Ask the pupil to fill in the missing words so the passage makes sense.
* Give comprehension questions before reading begins. Encourage the pupils to monitor what they are reading in relation to the questions that will be asked. This will help pupils to develop their awareness of the need to follow the meaning of the words as they read.

Visualising

* Pupils may not even realise that they can visualise a story. Talk to your pupils about turning what they read into a 'movie' in their heads as they read.
* Read aloud to the pupils and ask them to listen with their eyes closed, imagining the story in their minds.
* Encourage the pupils to draw a series of storyboards that tell the story in picture form.
* Watching a video or movie of the story before beginning to read can substantially improve pupils' abilities to visualise the story, relate to the characters and follow the plot.

Finding the right answer; formulating the right answer

* Ask your pupils to be detectives and locate where information is in the text. 'Find the words that tell us that the lion was getting annoyed. … Where does it give us a clue about what might happen next? … How do you know where the story is taking place? … What does the author tell us about Eloise and Harry?'
* Give explicit instruction in how to formulate an answer. Teach the pupils that a Why question usually needs because in the answer; Where is followed by an answer that includes mention of a place; When has to be answered with an indication of time and so on.
* Teach pupils to use the words from the question when they formulate an answer. This not only helps pupils to understand the correct way to respond to a formal question, but also provides an excellent starting point for the answer. For example, let's say the question is, 'Why do you think Rex went away without saying anything?' The pupil might respond in either of the following ways:

  ✗ 'He was scared'.
  ✓ 'Rex went away without saying anything because he was afraid of the boss'.

* Ask the pupils to read a passage and write their own set of comprehension questions. Pupils can exchange questions with each other or ask an adult the questions instead. It takes a strong understanding of what is read to be able to generate good questions.

✳ Give the pupils several possible answers to each comprehension question. Discuss with the pupils which answers work best and how poor answers could be improved.

Making the connections

✳ Give the pupils a context for what they are reading. If the book that your pupils are reading takes place in an unfamiliar time, situation or place, provide plenty of information that helps to set the scene for the pupils. Provide pictures, video or teaching content as a starting point.

✳ Make sure pupils with poor general knowledge or understanding are reading books that relate to familiar topics and situations, so the pupils can connect their current knowledge to what they are reading.

Pupil may have visual difficulties

Reading observation chart: section 10

10. Pupil may have visual difficulties

Pupil rubs eyes when reading

Pupil tilts head when reading

Pupil uses finger to keep place when reading

Pupil covers one eye with hand when reading

Pupil complains of headache when reading

Pupil skips words and lines when reading

Pupil reads for only a short period of time before needing a break

Pupil chooses books with large print

It is obvious that good eyesight is important for reading. Being able to read the doctor's eyesight chart does not mean the pupil has adequate vision for reading. The doctor's chart usually tests distance vision of single letters. To be able to read, pupils must be able to:

• see the words clearly when they are close, for example in a book
• see words clearly at a distance, for example on the board
• scan along a line of print, accurately moving from one section to the next
• drop down accurately to the beginning of the next line of print
• get both eyes to work together, so there is one sharp image, not two
• sustain focus on the print for a considerable period of time
• alternate focus, for instance, if they are reading from the board and then writing in their books

One last point to remember! Not all visual difficulties are completely corrected by glasses.

Strategies for managing visual Problems

Getting information about possible or known visual problems

✳ Monitor all pupils for signs of visual problems. Beware of simply asking pupils if they can see well. They may not realise that their vision is poor, as it is all they have ever known.

* Arrange for any pupil showing signs of visual difficulties to have a full test of vision if you are concerned about the pupil's reading. Make sure the specialist knows that reading and school work are of concern.
* If pupils have known visual problems, do not assume that because they wear glasses, they can see perfectly. Check with the pupil's specialist and/or the advisory teacher for visual impairment so that you can understand the nature of the pupil's visual difficulties and the impact this might have on the pupil's reading.
* If pupils do have known visual difficulties, check that their needs with regards to print size, lighting levels and visual aids are known and accommodated.

Making the classroom and school work vision friendly

* Make sure that the lighting in your classroom is good. Good illumination aids good vision and helps to prevent strain.
* Watch out for shadows. Even if the pupils are in good lighting, there is still a risk that shadows may fall on some work spaces.
* Make sure that your board has good lighting but is away from glare. Avoid using colours that have poor contrast with the background.
* Avoid seating pupils so they have to turn around 180 degrees to see the board and turn back to do their work.
* Make worksheets easy on the eye. *All* pupils benefit from worksheets, assignment sheets and test papers that are clearly presented. Avoid a visually cluttered sheet. Make sure that photocopying is clear. Choose a legible font. (Arial, 12 point is ideal.) Use clear graphics and formatting to make the page easy to understand.

Pupil has advanced reading skills

Reading observation checklist: section 11

11. Pupil has advanced reading skills

Pupil's reading is advanced in comparison to peer group.

Pupil complains that reading is boring, even though the pupil reads well

Pupil prefers factual books to fiction

In most classes, some pupils will have exceptionally advanced reading skills. Usually, their advanced reading skills will be a positive. Nevertheless, some consideration will also have to be given to these pupils' special needs. For example, the young pupil with advanced reading skills may not need to go through the series of graded readers that are necessary for most pupils. Preference for factual books rather than fiction may reflect some pupils' difficulties in finding intellectually stimulating material that does not rely on adult themes.

Strategies for supporting advanced reading skills

Individualising the reading programme

* If the pupil is already a competent reader, allow them to skip all (or some) of the graded readers.
* Pupils with advanced reading skills may not need to join in class or group instruction of skills such as word decoding using phonics. Give these pupils an alternative activity at this time.
* Provide a wide selection of books that are suitable for the pupil's reading level but which also match the pupil's emotional and social maturity. Allow the pupil to select freely from these books.

* Recognise that many pupils with advanced reading skills enjoy or prefer nonfiction reading. Make sure there is a wide range of nonfiction in the mix of books offered.
* Give the pupil with advanced reading skills reading lists that suggest clusters of reading arranged by genre, author, topic and so forth. This encourages the pupil to follow through from one book they have enjoyed to others of a similar type. For instance, the pupil might enjoy one biography and be interested in reading other biographies suggested on the reading list.
* Develop advanced reading comprehension skills and answering techniques. Encourage the pupil to move beyond a simple retelling of facts to interpreting, analysing and comparing. For example, instead of asking the pupil to describe the characters in the book, ask the pupil to compare and contrast two of the characters.

Placing the pupil in a stimulating reading environment

* Put advanced readers together in a reading group. The teacher may select the book for the group to read, or the pupils may take turns selecting titles. One pupil may be asked to present the book, for example, talking about the author and giving the group background information before the group discussion. Multiple copies of the book obviously have to be made available.

Concluding Chapter 2

This chapter has discussed difficulties that may arise for pupils as they learn how to read. It also has presented strategies for helping both pupils who are struggling and those who are unusually advanced for their age group. The awareness gained here should help in detecting the sources of reading difficulties, which will, in turn, help determine the best strategies to utilise. Many of the strategies given are appropriate for any young reader. Appropriate interventions will help to include all pupils in classroom reading activities and will thus support their self-esteem and attitude towards learning this most important life skill.

Chapter 3

Written language

Introduction

Difficulties with written language along with difficulties in reading are probably the two major reasons pupils feel discouraged and inadequate in the classroom.

Being able to produce good written language is, of course, a very important part of success at school and in the world beyond. What about the pupils who have difficulty putting their ideas on paper? Many are talented and knowledgeable, others less so. All, however, need to be able to share their ideas with others, both in speaking and in writing.

Some pupils may fail courses of study, or underachieve, because what they write does not reflect what they know. When assessment is based only on what a pupil can write, then of course pupils who find it difficult to express themselves in print will be disadvantaged.

> Bob is now a successful builder. He recalls: 'When I was a kid, I loved woodwork and metalwork and all that sort of thing. I was talented too. I could make anything you wanted. But then there were the exams, they were another story. I could have told you the answers, I could have shown you the answers, but writing them down? No way! Then one year I got lucky and broke my arm so I had to do the test verbally – straight A – and then the teachers could see that I was pretty knowledgeable about it all – it was just writing it down that was my downfall.'

In this chapter, we look at the difficulties that can arise with written language.

The section headings in this chapter follow the structure of Appendix Form 2: 'Written language observation chart'.

The chart may be photocopied and used to informally assess and record individual reading difficulties for pupils. This chart is divided into eight sections, with each focusing on a specific area of written language. As you assess individual pupils, specific patterns of difficulty may emerge. The sections in the chart will provide a direct link between the recorded written language observation chart and the corresponding strategies in this chapter that will help the pupil in the specific area(s) of need. The eight sections of the chart also have been reproduced within the main text of this chapter.

If you are interested in using the strategies without completing an informal assessment of the pupil, these sections will easily guide you through the chapter and provide a quick, easy reference tool for specific areas in reading. This will enable you to select from the intervention strategies, modifications and adaptations listed to help individual and small groups of pupils.

The following forms from the appendix are referred to in this chapter:

Appendix Form 2: 'Written language observation chart'
Appendix Form 37: 'Pupil reward cards'

Appendix Form 9:   'New ideas for writing'
Appendix Form 7:   'Spelling log'
Appendix Form 10: 'Punctuation checker'.

Pupil feels negative about writing

Written language observation chart: section 1

---

1. Pupil feels negative about writing

Pupil complains when asked to write

Pupil avoids writing whenever possible

Pupil's writing is very brief in comparison to peers' work.

Pupil expresses difficulty in knowing how to start or knowing what to write

---

Writing is a complex process involving ideas, language, spelling, handwriting, punctuation, etc. Pupils with difficulties often feel overwhelmed by having so many targets within one task.

> 'If I make it neat then I won't get much done. ... If I write this really great idea, I won't be able to spell the words. If I stop and fix the spelling, I'll forget what I'm writing about. I'll never get all that done. Maybe I'll write something short and get it finished.'

Writing also has the potential to expose the pupil to ridicule and embarrassment. Pupils often feel more comfortable with a worksheet that has a lot of structure. This helps to reassure the pupil that they are working along the right lines. But a blank piece of paper?

> 'What if what I write sounds dumb? Once I've written it down, I'm stuck with it. It might be wrong. I'm not so sure I know what she wants. ... I might have to read out loud what I've written and it will be stupid.'

Some pupils cannot make up their minds between several competing ideas and end up not even starting, because they are not sure which is 'right'. Pupils need to understand that writing is not a closed subject where there is only one 'right' answer.

Pupils may put a lot of effort and time into writing only to produce disappointing work. Some may find it hard to know what to write or how to get started. Others may have good ideas but lack the skill to get their ideas down on paper. Pupils may then feel discouraged and negative about writing.

> A parent explained: 'I watch him sit there, sometimes for hours, working away ... writing something down, scratching his head, chewing his pencil, altering what he has done. And after all that, he has – maybe – a quarter of a page of terrible writing that I can hardly make out. His teacher says that, at school, he often has to stay in at lunchtime to catch up with the work.'

Being slow and experiencing difficulties with written work may mean that some pupils seldom get to finish any piece of work to a satisfactory standard. Their books may contain half finished, poorly done written work. This does not build confidence or positive feelings towards writing. It is also a inappropriate work ethic to leave work unfinished and of limited quality.

Strategies for developing positive attitudes towards writing

Using multimedia

* Encourage all forms of communication in the classroom. Encourage pupils to talk, draw, act, build, demonstrate and share knowledge, so that they remain interested and positive about the task itself.
* Make writing part of an interesting task that has other, supplementary ways of covering the topic. For example, make a photo journal with written captions and explanatory paragraphs.
* Use technology, so pupils can use computer programs, cameras, recording and multimedia to help get their ideas across.

Providing support and guidance

* Provide appropriate intervention to improve pupils' skills. (See following sections.)
* Ensure that you use a range of inclusive strategies to make sure that the pupil is not at a disadvantage because of writing difficulties. (See following sections.)
* Brainstorm the task with the class before the pupils start to write. This will help trigger ideas and set the scene for the required assignment.
* Show pupils how different writers tackle the same topic in different ways. There can be several, quite different but equally acceptable, ways of tackling a writing assignment.
* Help pupils to choose between ideas or approaches by reminding them that other ideas can be tried at a later date.
* Give your class 'writing dash' as a regular activity. Set a very short time limit for the writing, so pupils learn to write whatever comes into their heads without stopping to worry about whether they are right or wrong. 'You have one minute to write about your favorite type of weather. Tell me why you like that weather best. …' or 'Here is the start of a story. You have five minutes to write the rest of the story.'
* Many pupils find it hard to get started with written work. Provide a few words or a sentence to get them started.
* Provide pupils with a scaffold for writing, such as a set of headings or an outline, to guide their writing and support their confidence.
* Let the pupils know your priorities for the task, so they will know where to direct their efforts. 'Today I am looking for really imaginative ideas, so we will not worry about neat writing or spelling right now.' Or 'This activity is for practice with handwriting and presentation, so take your time – and remember, I am looking for good handwriting and presentation as my number one priority.'
* Assign several short writing assignments for the whole class. Fast writers may complete several; slower writers just one or two.
* Allow time for slow writers to complete work over several days – not as a punishment, but as an acknowledgement that good writing is a process of evolution that may take time to complete.
* Do not display pupils' work to others unless they are comfortable with you doing so.

Valuing effort

*   Evaluate outcomes on the basis of the effort put into them. Value the best that pupils can do.
*   Emphasise the concept of 'personal best'. Developing writing skills is an ongoing process, so a small improvement in comparison to previous work should be celebrated as a real achievement.
*   Use Appendix Form 37: 'Pupil reward cards', or create your own cards with sayings, designs, stickers or the like to acknowledge pupils' efforts and further inspire them.
*   Make explicit and realistic goals for improvement in writing, so the pupil can see that the target goal is within reach.
*   Emphasise that, in writing, there can be many 'right' ways to do something.

Difficulties with written language impact classroom achievement

Written language observation chart: section 2

2. Difficulties with written language impact classroom achievement

Pupil's oral contribution in class is not reflected in written work

Pupil does not do well on written assignments, tests and exams

Pupil has problems in getting ideas down on paper

Pupil writes sentences that are brief, incomplete, disjointed or hard to follow

Pupil does not use a wide vocabulary to express ideas

Pupil often repeats words and sentences over and over again

Pupil often uses the same format in every type of writing

Pupil has difficulties in sequencing sentences in logical order

Pupils may underachieve with school work because they cannot fully show their understanding and knowledge when they write. They may be able to have a strong verbal discussion on a topic, answer questions well orally or give a good oral presentation to the class, but then fail to produce the same quality work when they write.

In tests and examinations, difficulties in getting ideas down on paper may be a major problem and seriously disadvantage the pupil.

The mechanics of writing may be difficult. The pupil may find it difficult to find the right words or put words together into a good sentence: 'We did went and Dad came over the night'.

The pupil may rely on the same set of words over and over again: 'We went to the park we went to our friends we went home'. Or the same sentence structure may be used over and over again: 'Bo liked Jane. Dad came home. I played ball.'

Even when pupils have mastered the basics of writing sentences, they may have difficulties in putting sentences together to connect pieces of writing. Collecting information from several sources and pulling it all together into a coherent whole can be a very challenging task.

Strategies for managing writing difficulties in the classroom

Using alternative assessments

*   Many writing assignments can also be done in other modalities. Look to see if the same assessment objective could be met in a different way, such as an oral presentation, a diagram or a chart.

* Some pupils may benefit from recording their own voices and then transcribing their own words.
* The use of voice recognition software can enable pupils to dictate directly onto a computer, while the computer types up their words. This usually requires the pupil to go through training process of 'teaching' the software to recognise the pupil's unique vocal characteristics.
* If knowledge is being tested, a multiple choice test where pupils 'check the box' may be a good substitute for a written examination.
* If the task requires the pupil to give a persuasive argument, an oral presentation may work as the assessment.
* Straightforward reporting of facts is also easily turned into an oral exercise. (Think how much of our daily news is delivered to us by audiovisual means as opposed to print media.)
* A pupil might construct a model, draw a series of cartoon strips or give a demonstration to illustrate a scientific principle.
* Use a combination of modalities, so a pupil can create a presentation that has only a small amount of written language supplemented by graphics, spoken word and dramatisation. For example, if the class has been given a history assignment on the Wars of the Roses, the pupil may create a series of imaginary news bulletins of the events as they unfold, with maps, captions, 'interviews' with key characters and so on.

Providing support

* Allow pupils to work in small teams, so skills can be combined. A pupil who can write well may benefit from the ideas and innovation of a pupil with writing difficulties. On the other hand, the pupil who does not write well benefits from the writing skills of the team member. Together, the team can produce a good piece of work.
* Provide a writing mentor for the pupil with difficulties. The mentor is available to provide discussion, guidance and practical advice while the pupil writes.

Using a scribe

* Have a scribe write down what a pupil wants to say as a substitute for a written assignment.
* Provide a quiet and private environment for the pupil to work with the scribe.
* Make sure that a scribe is available for tests and examinations.
* If pupils are to use scribes in an examination, make sure they are already familiar and confident with dictating their work well before the exam.
* When using scribes, encourage pupils to make notes, chart the ideas and prepare a framework before beginning. This helps to formulate their ideas.
* Allow pupils to use notes, charts, etc., in an exam as preparation for dictation to a scribe.
* When a pupil has dictated a piece of work, make sure there is an opportunity for the pupil to hear the work read back so that any necessary corrections can be made. If the pupil has reading difficulties, the scribe may read back the work to the pupil and insert the corrections as directed by the pupil.
* If scribes are to be used in a formal test or examination, make sure they take dictation without comment or input. They are acting as writing 'machines'. Obviously the scribe must be able to write or type quickly and legibly.

Developing creative writing

❋   Some pupils find it very difficult to write from their imagination. Offer the option of factual writing. For example, the pupil may do well writing a report about a real event or on a topic of scientific interest.

❋   Help pupils who find imaginative writing difficult to develop a real situation into something more creative. (See Table 3.1.)

❋   You can use Appendix Form 9 'New ideas for writing' to help the pupils expand their ideas for imaginative writing.

❋   Some pupils find creative writing very threatening. They are afraid that their ideas will sound silly. Brainstorm with a group of pupils to help them see that lots of ideas have merit and can work, even if they seem a bit far-fetched.

❋   Brainstorming can also help trigger ideas in those pupils who do not have great imaginations or many creative ideas.

❋   You can provide a story in cartoon form and ask pupils to retell the story in their own words. This is reassuring for those pupils who find it hard to create stories themselves.

❋   Provide structure and a framework for pupils who really find creative writing difficult. You may need to give them some 'factual' information about characters or events to get them started on their writing. For example: 'Write a story about three brothers who lived on a farm. The story should be about how the boys discovered something very unusual in the barn. Your story should include an exciting chase on horseback.'

❋   Assign a task where certain words and phrases have to be included in a story. For example: 'Write a story and include the following words. You can use the words in any order you like to make your story interesting and exciting. The words are: *house, hill, dark, storm, yellow eyes, river, bridge, police, amazing, chocolate cake, grandmother* and *biggest I had ever seen*.'

Developing written expression

❋   Develop the pupil's vocabulary. Take every opportunity to introduce new words and phrases. Read to your pupils and discuss unfamiliar words, talk to them and expand their vocabulary.

❋   Start a classroom list that contains new or unusual words. Ask pupils to look for words that will baffle their classmates – and even the teacher!

❋   Have activities where the pupils work with synonyms, antonyms and word meanings, and encourage them to use new words in their own writing: 'How many words can you think of to describe water falling down? It can gush, drip, pour, sprinkle, or tumble. How can you improve the sentence that says "It was raining".'

Table 3.1 Strategies for developing imaginative writing

Strategy to move from real to imaginary	Real facts	Imaginary or creative idea
Exaggerate	It was a hot day.	It was so hot that the road was melting.
Substitute	My sister went to church with me.	The dog came to church with me.
Reverse	Dad had to look for my little brother who was lost.	Dad got lost and we had to look for him.
Elaborate	We ate a hamburger.	We ate a juicy, sizzling hamburger with ketchup and fries.
Hypothesise	She was smiling.	I wondered if she had discovered the secret treasure.

✳ Ask pupils to revise early drafts to improve written expression. They can look for opportunities to vary sentence structure, replace simple words with more interesting ones and expand what they have written.

✳ Encourage pupils to look out for repetition of ideas. Often pupils are working with very few ideas, which are recycled over and over again. If this is the problem, ask questions, provide resource material and brainstorm in class to produce more ideas.

✳ Provide explicit teaching in sentence construction. Use formal activities to show pupils that language can be deliberately manipulated to make expression clearer. For example, ask pupils to try some of the following:
  • combine two simple sentences into one compound one
  • split a long sentence into two shorter sentences
  • turn a sentence into the past tense
  • make an active sentence passive
  • rewrite a story, changing from first person to third person.

✳ Have pupils experiment with 'voice': 'How would this story sound if the giant was telling it? What words would he use? What would it sound like if the old grandmother was telling it? How would she tell the story?'

Helping with planning and organising ideas

✳ Teach skills in planning for larger pieces of work. Encourage pupils to create a plan or create an outline before the pupil begins to write.

✳ Look at available software that helps to organise ideas.

✳ Use mind mapping to help pupils learn how to gather ideas and put them into logical clusters.

✳ Give direct instruction and practice on the skills of linking one idea with another.

✳ Ask pupils to build a glossary of linking words and phrases, such as *other people think that ... as a result of this ... soon after ... even though ... however ... eventually.*

✳ Provide pupils with a paragraph with the middle sentence removed. The pupils' task is to 'repair' the paragraph by writing a sentence that will link the remaining sentences in a logical way.

Pupil has spelling difficulties

Written language observation chart: section 3

---

3. Pupil has spelling difficulties

Pupil makes many spelling errors

Pupil makes phonological errors in spelling, such as *beg/bec*

Pupil does not use the correct letters for sounds, such as *train/tran*

Pupil makes errors in the use of spelling rules

Pupil has repeated spelling errors with common words, such as *what/wot*

Pupil's work is full of spelling corrections made as the pupil writes

Pupil successfully learns words for a spelling test but then forgets them

---

Spelling can prove to be a difficult and frustrating aspect of writing for many pupils. Good spelling depends on the pupil having:

  • good phonological skills (the ability to break spoken words into a sequence of sounds)
  • the capacity to remember the letters that represent sounds
  • the ability to recall visual sequences

- solid knowledge in spelling rules and word construction
- good 'motor memory' for spelling patterns in handwriting and typing
- the ability to retain spelling patterns that have been learned by rote.

We often give pupils spelling words to learn at the beginning of the week and a final test on Friday. It is then assumed that the ability to spell those words will stay with the pupil forever. It is an interesting assumption that pupils need only four days to learn a spelling word and then will remember it forever!

Many pupils can do well on the Friday spelling test. However, they may immediately forget the words once the test is over. The pupil develops a regular 'learn and forget' cycle. The pupil learns new words for the next test but forgets the words that were learned the week before.

Pupils may be able to spell words in a list when the words are given slowly, one at a time. However, writing the same words correctly in context can prove to be much harder. Once the pupil's attention is diverted to producing good content, neat handwriting and so on, they may not be able to concentrate on spelling as well.

Skilled spellers have a repertoire of words that they can spell automatically. However, even very skilled spellers also use phonological skills surprisingly often, quickly making a mental reference to the way the word sounds and then adjusting the spelling accordingly.

Pupils with phonological difficulties may be unsure of the speech patterns in a word and so make errors such as writing *house* as *hals*. They may be able to work out some phonological patterns, but only with slow, careful analysis.

Remembering the link between letters and sounds can be very challenging, especially when the pupil has to remember groups of letters that make new sounds. Pairs of letters that create a sound identical to a letter name, such as *ai, ar,* or *ie,* can be particularly confusing.

Good spellers can often look at a word and know on the basis of its appearance that it is not right. Sometimes they can tell how to correct the error right away, and sometimes they need to keep writing versions down until they find the one that looks right. However, some pupils cannot tell that a word looks wrong. They can write version after version without coming across one that looks right.

Many pupils who have spelling difficulties find it hard to use a dictionary. They may not know the order of the alphabet well enough to find the initial letter. Perhaps their spelling is so off track that they do not know where to start to find the right word (for example, searching under *w* for the word *once*). Even if they determine the first letter, what is the next letter? And the letter that comes after that? Sometimes you really need to be able to spell the word to be able to find it in the dictionary!

Pupils who find it hard to remember the appearance of words may have persistent difficulty with commonly used words.

When teaching spelling, we need to remember that there are two types of words. Some words have a regular phonic pattern, and you can sound them out. Referring back to the sequence of sounds in the word helps pupils to remember these words.

Other words are irregular. These words will not sound out. A multi-sensory approach that reinforces a 'motor memory' helps pupils remember these words.

Strategies for working with spelling difficulties

Encouraging quality writing

✱ Separate good and creative writing skills from the actual spelling of words. Give credit for interesting, creative writing, even when spelling is poor.
✱ Encourage pupils to write freely, using invented spelling, if necessary. Assist the pupil with corrections after the first draft has been completed.

✳ Encourage the use of a word processor to provide support with spelling.
✳ Ensure that the program is customised correctly if there are options for spelling.
✳ For pupils with severe spelling difficulties, consider the use of a software program that has predictive text.
✳ For pupils with extreme spelling difficulties, consider the use of voice activated word processing.

Providing support in the classroom

✳ In the classroom, provide a range of resources to assist pupils with spelling. Some examples include:
  • charts of commonly used words and phrases
  • posters of common spelling patterns
  • spelling rules (with examples) clearly displayed
  • lists of topic words for the current classroom project
  • personal dictionaries at a suitable level of difficulty
  • electronic spell checkers and dictionaries
  • classroom dictionaries.
✳ Provide pupils with spelling difficulties with a personal 'desk dictionary'. This is a single sheet or card, placed on the pupil's desk. The card has a list of all the commonly used words that the pupil cannot yet spell. The list changes regularly. When words are mastered, they are removed from the list. Other words can be inserted. Reminders about spelling rules and other writing formalities can also be included on the card as needed.
✳ Arrange for a 'spelling partner' to be available to help the pupil with spelling difficulties.
✳ Make sure that pupils with spelling difficulties develop good typing and word processing skills, so they can use a computer from an early age.
✳ Give pupils with spelling difficulties priority access to a computer for written language.
✳ Provide adult support for checking spelling during writing sessions.
✳ If the pupil has severe difficulties with spelling, have someone else type up the rough draft and make corrections in consultation with the pupil.
✳ Display a few irregular words in the classroom each week and give the pupils a challenge. Can they write for the whole week without ever making a mistake on these target words?

Teaching dictionary skills

✳ Provide regular practice at putting words in alphabetical order. Use a simple, illustrated dictionary to get started.
✳ Practice looking up names in a telephone directory for extra work with alphabetical order.
✳ Use address books with clearly marked alphabetical sections in which to write words that are needed as the pupil writes.
✳ Arrange for the pupil to store alphabetical index cards in a box for individual spelling words.
✳ Place alphabet tabs on the edge of dictionary pages to help pupils navigate their way through the dictionary.
✳ Teach pupils with severe spelling difficulties how to use an electronic rather than a paper dictionary.

Individualising the spelling programme

✳ Look at pupils' spelling difficulties in their free-style writing. Analyse the types of errors that occur. Look for the following patterns of error:
  • the use of the phonetic version of irregular words, such as *hir* instead of *here*
  • spelling the same word a different way each time it is used
  • losing track of the phonological pattern of the word, such as *but* for *boat*
  • failing to use spelling rules.
  Plan your teaching programme on the basis of the error patterns identified.

✳ 'More of the same' is not always a good intervention strategy for spelling difficulties. If the pupil is finding it difficult to learn and retain spelling, examine your teaching method and the way in which the pupil is learning. See if an alternative approach might work better.

✳ If the spelling list is too difficult for the pupil to learn within a few days, then the words are too hard. Place the pupil on a modified programme.

✳ Have differentiated spelling tasks for your class, so all pupils have words to learn that are appropriate to their own levels of achievement.

✳ If a pupil has difficulties with spelling, teach only new words that are certain to be used within the next few weeks. Words that are not used frequently will soon be forgotten.

✳ No pupil should ever have to learn to spell words they cannot read. If a pupil cannot read a word on the spelling list, remove that word from the list.

✳ Follow through after words have been tested. Use dictation, review spelling activities and even retest several times over the next few months.

✳ Avoid teaching words grouped according to themes. Cluster words that have a relationship with each other because of phonic pattern, derivation or other logical link.

Teaching irregular words (words that cannot be sounded out)

✳ Use rainbow writing. Ask the pupils to write the word in large letters and then use different coloured pencils to go over and over the letters to develop a motor memory of the spelling pattern.

✳ Irregular words often need a lot of over-learning before mastery occurs. So teach, practice, review and use the words over and over again. You can use Appendix Form 7: Spelling log to keep track of spelling mastery, see Table 3.2.

✳ Give individual pupils their own personal challenge words that they persistently spell incorrectly.

✳ Have pupils say the letters out loud as they write them down, and give repeated practice in doing this.

✳ Have pupils 'write' the words with 'sky writing'. They trace the spelling of the word in the air with a finger.

✳ If pupils are using cursive writing, encourage them to write their spelling words in cursive, as this helps to build motor memory.

✳ If pupils have handwriting difficulties, encourage them to type the words over and over again to consolidate the motor memory of the action of typing the word.

✳ Combine spelling and typing practice, using spelling words in typing tasks.

✳ Have pupils make a design of individual words, decorating the shapes.

✳ Talk to pupils about spelling patterns: 'Look at this word. It says *who*. Which letter is the silent letter? There is something weird about the *oo* sound. How is it spelled in this word? If we mix the letters around, can we make another word?'

✳ Have the pupils make up their own memory prompts, or suggest some to them. For example, the first letters of the sentence *Big elephants can always understand small elephants* will spell the word *because*.

Table 3.2 Sample spelling log

Target word **weather**											
Daily practice until five consecutive ✓s are obtained	Date 3/2	Date 4/2	Date 5/2	Date 6/2	Date 7/2	Date 10/2	Date 11/2	Date 12/2	Date 13/2	Date 14/2	Date 17/2
✓ if correct, ✗ if incorrect	✗	✓	✓	✗	✓	✗	✓	✓	✓	✓	✓
Weekly practice until four consecutive ✓s are obtained	Date	Date	Date	Date	Date	Date	Date	Date	Date	Date	Date
✓ if correct, ✗ if incorrect	✓	✓	✓	✗	✓	✓	✓	✓			
Monthly practice until three consecutive ✓s are obtained	Date	Date	Date	Date	Date	Date	Date	Date	Date	Date	Date
✓ if correct, ✗ if incorrect	✓	✓	✓								

�✳ Teach 'old way–new way', if pupils are stuck with an incorrect spelling. 'You used to write *whent*. That was the old way. In the new way, you leave out *h* and write *went*.'

Teaching phonetic and pattern words

✳ Work on phonological awareness, so pupils learn and understand how to break down words into sounds.

✳ Have pupils say the sounds before they write the word.

✳ Teach reading and spelling together, so learning in reading crosses over and helps with spelling. Always teach a phonic skill in reading before the same skill is taught in spelling. For example if the pupil has just read a book containing the phonic words *ham, am, jam* then these are good spelling words too.

✳ Teach words in a sequence, so that phonics skills build gradually. This is exactly the same sequence as teaching reading using phonics (see Table 3.3).

✳ If pupils find it difficult to hear sounds in words, start by using plastic letters. Give only the letters they need for a word, and ask them to make the word. For example, give them the letters *i, g* and *p*, and ask them to put the letters together to make the word *pig*.

✳ Once pupils can build words using the letters, it is time for a bigger challenge. Give the pupils all the letters needed plus some extra letters, so they have to discriminate the sounds and choose the correct letters.

✳ Teach pupils to swap sounds to spell new words. For example, ask pupils: 'If this word says *log*, how can you change it to say *hog*?'

✳ Use nonsense words to extend practice in listening to the sounds in a word and writing the 'word' down.

✳ Teach words together that share the same phonetic pattern, so pupils see the link. For example, introduce *beach, peach, teach, reach* as a group.

Table 3.3 Sequence for teaching phonic spelling patterns

Stage 1	Use words in the consonant-vowel-consonant pattern. For example *set, pet, wet* or *pin, win, tin, bin* or *fat, cat, hat*. Notice that often these words can be clustered in groups that share the same vowel-consonant ending (called the rime) but have different initial letters (called the onset). Teaching onset-rime patterns makes this first stage much easier, as learning from one word can be generalised to the next. If you can spell *pin*, it is easy to spell *win*.
Stage 2	Two consonants slide together. For example, *trip, spin, stop*. Two consonants make a new sound. For example, *ship, chop, thin*. Final *e*. For example, *hope, take, like*. Use a maximum of four letters in each word, so the pupil only has to deal with one letter blend.
Stage 3	Two vowels make a new sound. For example *out, feet, boat*. Vowel and consonant make a new sound. For example, *part, dawn, dirt*. Silent letters. For example, *gnaw, knot*.
Stage 4	Three consonants slide together. For example, *shrug, strap, scream*. Four letters make a new sound. For example, *ration, light, rough*. Words ending in *y* or *ing*. For example, *happy, silly, tapping, ring*.
Stage 5	Words that combine two or more of the previously taught patterns. For example, *combine, sprout, market* Words that are compound words, words using prefixes or suffixes. For example, *preview, unhappy, defeat*

Pupil has handwriting difficulties

Written language observation chart: section 4

4. Pupil has handwriting difficulties

Pupil does not always form letters correctly

Pupil's letters and words are often too close together, have irregular spacing or are too widely spaced

Pupil prints instead of using cursive writing

Pupil's writing begins neatly but quickly becomes messy

Pupil takes longer than peers to complete writing tasks, and work is still untidy

Pupil's hand gets tired or sweaty after a few minutes of writing

Some pupils experience significant difficulty with handwriting. This can cause considerable frustration by limiting the quantity and quality of the written work that the pupil can produce.

Handwriting is a complex neurological process. Messages have to travel from the brain to the hand in a continuous flow. The muscles of the hand have to respond to these messages with speed and accuracy, and in sequence. For some pupils, this process does not work well.

It is tempting to assume that the pupil can easily improve handwriting skills by taking more time or practising more. However, this is often a false assumption. Most handwriting difficulties are neurological dysfunctions. These difficulties will not necessarily respond well to increased levels of practice, especially in the older pupil who has been practicing for many years.

Some pupils can write neatly for a short period of time, particularly if they can take their time and write at their own pace. However, sustained writing is quite a different matter. Some pupils will write the first sentence quite well, but their writing rapidly deteriorates as time goes by. A rest break may restore neatness for a few minutes before the cycle begins all over again.

Other pupils may always have difficulties with neatness, and second or even third attempts may be little better than their first efforts. Handwriting may not reflect the effort put in. A huge effort might produce a short piece of written work that is neater, but the cost in terms of time and effort may be very high.

Strategies for managing handwriting difficulties

Modifying requirements and providing support

* Allow pupils plenty of time to write.
* Allow extra time in tests and examinations to compensate for slow writing.
* Provide a scribe to take dictation from the pupil.
* Allow the pupil to do an oral rather than a written assignment.
* Allow rest breaks, if sustained writing is a problem during class work or tests.
* Give credit for content of what the pupil writes, rather than handwriting or presentation.
* Accept that if work is done quickly, then it may be very untidy.
* Minimise unnecessary writing. Provide lesson notes, handouts, copies, worksheets and so forth to help reduce the amount of writing required.
* Modify tests to reduce the amount of handwriting required. For example, use a multiple-choice format instead of an essay.
* Allow the pupil to make corrections to a handwritten draft using an eraser or whiteout rather than have the pupil rewrite the piece of work.
* Remember that untidy writing does not necessarily mean that the pupil has been careless or lazy.
* Encourage the pupil to experiment with different types of pens or pencils. Allow the pupil to use the one that suits them best.
* Do not require pupils to rewrite work because it is untidy, unless you are certain that they can easily do better.
* Recognise that pupils may be able to produce neat work under special circumstances, but that they cannot maintain that standard for all work every day.
* The desk and chair should be the right height for the pupil.
* Pupils should have good writing posture. The pupil should not be slouching and should have both feet on the ground and back supported by the chair.

Using computers

* Encourage the pupil with a handwriting difficulty to use a word processor instead of handwriting.
* Do not ask pupils to do a handwritten draft before they type their work up. Encourage them to develop the skill of typing the first draft on the computer.
* Some pupils with handwriting problems also find typing difficult. Try using voice recognition software as an alternative to typing.
* Have an adult type the rough draft for the pupil.

Pupil finds it difficult to copy accurately

Written language observation chart: section 5

5. Pupil finds it difficult to copy accurately

Pupil makes errors when copying words

Pupil needs additional time to complete copying as compared to peers

Some pupils have quite marked difficulties in copying things down. They may write very slowly. They find it hard to remember the appearance of words that they cannot already spell. They may also have to constantly refer back and forth between the book and the paper.

Strategies for managing copying difficulties

Providing support

* Provide handouts instead of having the pupil copy large amounts of material.
* Allow extra time when copying is essential.
* Allow pupils to take photocopies or scan rather than copying things by hand.
* Ask a fellow pupil to make a carbon copy of the notes.
* Leave notes on display until all pupils have had time to copy them.
* Arrange the desks and tables so that pupils are facing the board. Avoid having pupils with their backs, or even sides, to the board during copying exercises.
* Place important information on the school or class website, so pupils can access it at any time.
* Provide worksheets instead of having pupils copy exercises from the textbooks.
* Check that the pupil has copied correctly when taking down important information (such as details of a homework assignment or a school field trip).
* Request to have a pupil's eyesight checked, if they seem to have trouble seeing the board.
* Have pupils use a strip of firm cardboard or a ruler under the line of text they are copying.

Pupil has difficulties with punctuation

Written language observation chart: section 6

6. Pupil has difficulties with punctuation
Pupil makes errors in punctuation when writing spontaneously
Pupil makes more errors than peers when doing formal punctuation

Punctuation is an important, but often neglected, aspect of writing. As adults, we know that punctuation is needed to give shape to what the writer has to say. Skilled writers use punctuation to add an extra dimension to what they write. It can even change the meaning of a sentence!

Strategies for working with punctuation

Improving punctuation and formatting

* Give explicit instruction about punctuation, and revisit the basics at frequent intervals.

Areas to look for:	Checked
Correct punctuation at the end of sentences	

* Give instruction in how punctuation is used when reading out loud. Once pupils understand this, punctuating their own work is easier.
* Provide formal assignments that are focused on punctuation and formatting.

❋ Provide the pupil with a checklist for punctuation, and go through the steps before the pupil begins to write. Highlight areas where the pupil has specific difficulties. You can use Appendix Form 10 'Punctuation checker', or create your own.

Areas to look for:	Checked
Capital letters at beginning of sentences	
Capitalised proper nouns	
Question marks	
Quotation marks	
Commas	
Paragraphs	
Personal points to watch	

❋ Nominate another pupil as a 'punctuation partner,' who will give advice if the pupil has a punctuation question.
❋ Encourage pupils to read their own work out loud and check the punctuation where there are pauses, emphases, questions, or stops.
❋ Give pupils a printed passage that has all punctuation removed. Read the passage aloud, and ask the pupils to fill in the punctuation.

Pupil has difficulties with proofreading and editing

Written language observation chart: section 7

7. Pupil has difficulties with proofreading and editing
Pupil overlooks errors when proofreading
Teachers often comment, 'Check your work carefully'
Pupil may alter correct words during proofreading activities
Pupil may replace one error with another one during proofreading
Pupil is not able to describe or demonstrate strategies for proofreading
Pupil's editing of drafts leaves a significant number of unresolved problems
Pupil is not able to describe or evaluate personal writing strategies
Pupil does not seek editorial advice or assistance

Pupils who experience difficulties with written language often fail to check their work once finished. Maybe they are so glad to reach the end of the task that they want to leave it then and there! However, these same pupils often have genuine problems in recognising errors they have made.

Often the pupil may have checked their work but overlooked many of the mistakes. Sometimes a correct word has been deleted and replaced with an incorrect one.

Editing is an advanced skill that many pupils lack. Being able to review what you have written and correct not only spelling and punctuation but also expression, sentence structure and overall format is a demanding skill.

Strategies for helping with proofreading and editing

Providing support

* Provide pupils with in-class proofreading and editing assistance.
* Allow enough time for pupils to submit work, have it checked, and rework it.
* Have each pupil nominate an editor for their work. This can be a parent, friend, sibling, neighbour or teacher. The editor is asked to review each piece of written work. The work is signed including the editor's name; for example, 'Written by Sacha Davies, edited by Louise Alpin'.
* Teachers should give the editors a workshop at the beginning of the school year. The workshop should clarify that editors are advisors and consultants. The editor should understand that the pupil is the author of the work. The editor should not write or rewrite anything on the pupil's behalf, although they can suggest when changes or improvements are required.
* Give plenty of time for work to be written, to allow for several drafts and rewrites.
* Encourage pupils to get started as soon as possible with a writing task. Many pupils leave tasks until the last moment, allowing no time write a draft or to edit or rewrite the paper.
* Ensure that all pupils understand that writing is a craft and that most work needs to be revised, polished and carefully edited before it is finished.
* Create writing groups, where pupils read each other's drafts and then discuss each piece of work as an editorial panel. A teacher may facilitate the discussion. Obviously, the group must understand that the purpose of the group is positive, mutual support.

Building skills

* Look at the pattern of errors with the pupil, so the pupil understands the sort of mistakes that frequently occur. This helps the pupil become aware of the errors that need special attention as they write.
* Get pupils to write themselves a note for the start of the next piece of work. For instance, if they have left out capital letters in today's work, have them write 'Remember Capitals' on the top of the page where they will start tomorrow's writing.
* Provide a checklist for spelling and punctuation errors that will act as a reminder for the type of errors that frequently occur. The pupil will take particular care to watch out for these errors next time. Appendix Form 10 'Punctuation checker' may be personalised for individual pupils to include specific check points.

Watch out for these:	Checked
Ends of words	
Said not siad	
Capitals for proper nouns	

* Provide copies of real pupils' work. (Exchange with a colleague in another school or class.) Remove any identifying marks so the work is anonymous. Have your pupils proofread and edit the work. It is much more fun finding mistakes in other pupils' work!
* Ask a professional writer to come and talk to the pupils about how to go about writing and editing.
* Have pupils maintain a log of the drafting process, noting the date, the stage the work is in (e.g., Draft 2) and the editor's name.
* Have pupils keep the drafts on file. They should number each draft and submit it with the final piece of work.

* Encourage pupils to use 'track changes' in their computer program to show how their writing developed.
* If time allows, have pupils put the piece of work away and look at it again with fresh eyes a day or so later.
* Ask pupils to double space their work, so they (or their editors) have space to insert comments if necessary.
* Have pupils keep notes or a log on how editing changed their work. These notes can be used as a reference point for future writing. For example: 'I made the long sentences into two shorter sentences. I added some more descriptive words to make it more interesting. I rewrote the introductory paragraph to make it more exciting.'

Pupil has advanced writing skills

Written language observation chart: section 8

---

8. Pupil has advanced writing skills

Pupil sometimes produces work of exceptional quality

Pupil expresses a love of writing and will write by choice at home or at school

Pupil has accurate and advanced spelling skills

Pupil uses a wide range of vocabulary and expression.

Pupil uses punctuation accurately and to good effect

Pupil can vary writing style to meet various requirements

Pupil shows exceptional imagination and creativity in writing

---

Some pupils have exceptional writing capabilities, and they, too, will need special consideration so they are able to develop their talents to their full potential.

These pupils may have advanced vocabulary and background knowledge, they may be creative and imaginative, or they may love to research and write about factual topics, such as historical events or current affairs.

Strategies for developing advanced writing skills

Modifying the classroom programme

* Differentiate the classroom tasks, so the pupil with advanced writing skills can develop skills at a more complex level. For instance, if all pupils are assigned to write an account of their weekend activity, the more advanced pupil may try writing in a style other than first person. The pupil may write the account in the third person, as a travelogue, as a news report or perhaps in a poem.
* Group together the pupils who enjoy writing. Encourage these pupils to collaborate on challenging writing tasks, such as writing a class newspaper.
* Many pupils who write well are quite ambitious about what they want to write. Allow pupils to work on the same piece of work for several days, if not weeks, if they are keen to do so. Maintain a working plan of what they are doing.
* Watch out for capable pupils 'dumbing down' to fit in with the rest of the class. Challenge and provide extensions and encouragement for these pupils, so they continue to develop their talents.

Placing the pupil in a stimulating writing environment

* Set up a writers' group where pupils can bring their writing, learn new writing skills and enjoy each other's writing.

* Find someone who can mentor the pupils with advanced writing skills, so the pupils can explore the many exciting aspects of writing.
* Encourage pupils to submit their writing to literary magazines and competitions.

Concluding Chapter 3

This chapter has pointed out the many aspects involved in writing, such as spelling, punctuation, handwriting and written expression. Writing can be even more daunting to some pupils than reading. They are asked to put their thoughts and efforts down in concrete form to be 'judged', and many have a fear of being 'wrong'. The varied strategies suggested here provide support for pupils who have difficulties with writing as well as encouragement for those who are especially talented.

Chapter 4

Mathematics

Introduction

Did you know there are ten times as many books on literacy difficulties as there are on mathematics difficulties? Why is this so? Mathematics and literacy difficulties are equally common. So we would expect about the same level of interest (and book buying) in both topics. Perhaps mathematics is seen as less important than literacy. Or, maybe having difficulties with mathematics is accepted as 'normal', leading to less need for books on the topic. For whatever reason, mathematics does seem to be a relatively neglected area of intervention. However, mathematics is very important for inclusiveness throughout our lives.

In school, pupils who find mathematics difficult may be disadvantaged in a number of ways. They may not be able to participate fully in the regular classroom mathematics programme. Self-esteem and confidence may fall. The pupils' potential to succeed in subjects such as science and technical subjects may be reduced. In later years, they may be excluded from some courses of study because of poor mathematics results.

Today's pupils will all need mathematics when they leave school and get a job. All work places have some need for mathematics, such as timesheets, travel records, taking inventories and so on. Some pupils will need to have specific vocational mathematics to work in jobs such as woodworking, metalwork, cooking or banking. Others, of course, will need to use mathematics at a high level for engineering, science and the like.

All pupils will also need a basic competence in mathematics to cope with everyday adult life. Without an understanding of mathematics, the pupils will be disadvantaged to the end of their days. They will always need the skills and the confidence to make good decisions about wages, insurance, loans or any number of other financial transactions.

This chapter deals with the teaching of basic mathematics concepts and skills. Building interest and confidence in mathematics is also seen as an important element in intervention and inclusion.

The section headings in this chapter follow the structure of Appendix Form 3: 'Mathematics observation chart'. The mathematics observation chart may be photocopied and used to informally assess and record individual mathematics difficulties for pupils. The chart is divided into seven sections, each focusing on a specific area of mathematics. As you assess individual pupils, specific patterns of difficulty may emerge. The sections in the chart will provide a direct link between the recorded mathematics observation chart and the corresponding strategies in this chapter that will help the pupil in the specific area(s) of need. The seven sections of the chart have also been reproduced within the main this chapter.

If you are interested in using the strategies without completing an informal assessment of the pupil, these sections will easily guide you through the chapter and provide a quick, easy reference tool for specific areas in mathematics. This will enable you to select from the intervention strategies, modifications and adaptations listed to help individuals and small groups of pupils.

The following forms from the appendix are referred to in this chapter:

Appendix Form 3:   'Mathematics observation chart'
Appendix Form 41:   'Parent guide to mathematics at home'
Appendix Form 12:   'Addition chart'
Appendix Form 13:   'Subtraction chart'
Appendix Form 15:   'Mathematics checklist: addition (single-digit numbers)'
Appendix Form 19:   'Mathematics checklist: addition (two, two-digit numbers, no regrouping)'
Appendix Form 20:   'Mathematics checklist: addition (two, two-digit numbers, with regrouping)'
Appendix Form 16:   'Mathematics checklist: subtraction (single-digit numbers)'
Appendix Form 21:   'Mathematics checklist: subtraction (two-digit numbers, no exchanging)'
Appendix Form 22:   'Mathematics checklist: subtraction (two-digit numbers, with exchanging)'
Appendix Form 17:   'Mathematics checklist: multiplication'
Appendix Form 18:   'Mathematics checklist: division'
Appendix Form 11:   'Counting chart'
Appendix Form 14:   'Multiplication Chart'.

Pupil feels negative about mathematics

Mathematics observation chart: section 1

1. Pupil feels negative about mathematics

Pupil expresses dislike of mathematics

Pupil lacks confidence in own ability to solve mathematics problems

Pupil does not think mathematically in everyday situations

Pupil expresses having difficulty with mathematics

Pupil's mathematics difficulties impact the pupil's classroom achievements

Pupil needs additional time to complete mathematics tasks compared to peers

The language of mathematics may seem confusing

Literacy surrounds children in their everyday lives. The writing on a birthday card, the words on the television screen and many other forms of print prepare even the youngest child to understand that written letters represent words. Often children have an easy transition into school-based literacy learning.

But what about mathematics ? Although children will often learn about counting and written numbers before they start school, once in school, they are introduced to a whole new set of ideas, words and symbols. Mathematics can often seem much less familiar and less user-friendly than the written word. The words and symbols used can be difficult for pupils to grasp, and many misunderstandings can occur. For example, one pupil was quite sure that her teacher had said that the = sign was called *eagles* instead of *equals*!

It may seem 'normal' to find mathematics difficult

We often accept that mathematics is 'hard' and that it is quite 'normal' for a pupil to have difficulties with the subject. In turn, this may mean that some parents and teachers are quite complacent about the pupils' difficulties. It may also be that we do not expect pupils to enjoy mathematics.

If we assume that the difficulties are natural, we may not consider the need for appropriate intervention or special arrangements for inclusion.

Sometimes it is even felt that mathematics is a boys' subject. Expectations of what girls can achieve in mathematics may then be lowered. Girls may not be offered support to increase their mathematics performance.

Parents may find it hard to help with mathematics at home

Parents are often eager to help their children learn, however they may not know how to build mathematics into their child's daily routine. Often they understand mathematics as counting and learning basic mathematics facts. They may try to introduce their young child to formal algorithms in the hope that this will give them a head start in mathematics at school. Inappropriate 'help' at home can have a negative impact on a pupil's confidence in mathematics.

Mathematics is less flexible than literacy

In literacy, you can often get by with only partial understanding or mastery. For instance, you might be able to make some sense of a story even if you can't read all the words, or you could try to write a letter even if you're not sure how to spell all the words. Mathematics is often less flexible and less open-ended. Often, very definite levels of understanding and skills are required for satisfactory completion of the task.

Pupils can become defensive, defeated and distressed when they are not sure of what to do in mathematics.

Understanding difficulties in mathematics can be a challenge

It can be hard for pupils to say what is puzzling them. Asking for help or identifying what needs further explanation depends on the pupil having a reasonable grasp of the topic to begin with. One of the pupils' biggest challenges in mathematics is to explain what it is that they need help understanding. 'I don't know what I don't understand. All I know is I just don't get it.'

It can also be hard for the teacher to work out what is wrong! One of the teacher's biggest challenges is to locate where, within the concept or process, the pupil's understanding has failed. 'I went over the whole explanation again, and he still didn't get it.'

Mathematics skills build like a pyramid

Each step in mathematical understanding usually builds on the previous one in a pyramid fashion and links into other concepts in a logical way. Obviously, it is essential that these mathematics concepts and methods are taught and understood in a definite sequence. A pupil can easily lose track of an entire sequence of connected ideas. A few days away from school, a few inattentive minutes or difficulties understanding one concept or skill can break the pupil's grasp of a sequence of connected ideas. What was becoming clear can suddenly become incomprehensible, when just one, perhaps very small, piece of the puzzle is missing.

> 'I only missed a week from school, but when I got back they were doing decimals, and it seemed like they were on a different planet. It was years before I really understood what it was all about. I lost my confidence and went from being good at mathematics to being very average.'

Pupils vary in their position in the 'pyramid' of mathematics skills. Some pupils will find mathematics easy to learn, and others will find it much harder. Some will have had excellent groundwork from previous teachers; others may not be so fortunate. Your inclusive classroom will, of course, make allowances for a wide range of individual differences in mathematics experience and ability.

Good teaching is important

Good teaching is particularly important in mathematics, because the subject is so dependent on hierarchies of learning. Clear instruction and supervised practice at each stage is vital in laying down the foundations for successful learning. Even pupils with natural ability can become confused and frustrated by poor teaching. It is not unusual for pupils to do poorly one year and to excel the next, depending on the quality of the teaching they have received. Although some pupils do find mathematics easier than others, mathematics is a curriculum area where good teaching can make a substantial difference in the level of performance that pupils achieve.

Pupils may find some mathematics easy, other mathematics difficult

Although we refer to mathematics as if it were a single subject, it is a collection of diverse concepts and topics. Pupils who may have an aptitude for one type of mathematics, such as problem solving, might have difficulty in another area, such as mental computation.

Having difficulties with mathematics can create anxiety and undermine performance

Anxiety and frustration disrupt clear thinking. Negative emotions, such as anxiety, anger and frustration, can have a very damaging impact on mathematics learning.

Calm, systematic thinking is essential for success in mathematics. Unfortunately, this type of thinking is very quickly disrupted by anxiety or frustration. The pupil can very rapidly fall into a negative spiral. A small difficulty creates an emotional response, which disrupts thinking and compounds the problem. This leads to more emotion and an ever-widening spiral of difficulty.

> 'I knew I had made a mistake, but when I tried to check my work, my head went into a whirl and I couldn't think straight. I looked at the numbers, but they didn't make any sense at all. I knew it all so well, but I couldn't think clearly.'

Pupils 'switch off' when mathematics does not seem relevant

Perhaps the greatest barrier to successful mathematics learning is lack of apparent relevance and connection to everyday life. Many pupils will say they only do mathematics in a mathematics lesson in their mathematics books.

We all learn best when we see the relevance of what we learn. Learning is even easier when we find it interesting and reasonably easy. For many pupils, mathematics seems irrelevant, boring and difficult. Mathematics can often be done without any understanding of the process or its relevance to anything else. We have probably all known pupils who can calculate pages and pages of correct addition without having any idea of how this skill would be of use or interest to them in their daily lives. Many pupils develop a negative mindset, because they fail to see the purpose and value of mathematics in school.

Pupils have different interests and mindsets. Some are naturally drawn towards mathematics, other prefer social topics, art, sports, creating, music and so on. Making connections between mathematics and the pupils' personal interests is often the key to making mathematics relevant and interesting.

Some pupils find it difficult to relate the mathematics skills and concepts learned in school to real-life situations. For example, a pupil may use counting blocks in school to work out the answer to a problem but never think of using blocks or counters in a real-life setting.

Belle's mother explained: 'You know, she has the numbers right up to 100 in the classroom, up there on the wall, and she seems OK with them. But when I tried to show her how to use my tape measure at home, she just didn't get it.'

Strategies for making mathematics a positive experience

Teaching the language of mathematics

* Use everyday language and real-life examples alongside the technical words and formal methods when you teach mathematics. Help your pupils understand that mathematics is an extension of ordinary, everyday activities.
* Use mathematics concepts and language whenever you can. Make opportunities for the pupils to think mathematically in general classroom activities. Use the words and ideas from the mathematics curriculum in other settings, too. Here are some ideas to get you started:
  * We have used up half the paint. That's 50 per cent used up and 50 per cent left for the next job.'
  * 'Two pupils are absent today, so 28 minus 2 is 26. That means we have a total of 26 pupils here today.'
  * 'We have five boys and nine girls. That's not equal! How many girls have to go over to the boys' side to make the numbers equal?'
  * 'Let's divide these up equally between you.'
* Take extra care that all pupils understand new mathematical words and symbols. Discuss the new words and symbols, and ask pupils to show their understanding with practical demonstrations.
  * 'What other words do we know that mean the same as "plus"?'
  * 'Take these beans and show me what three times four looks like.'
  * 'Put the total number of balls in the basket.'
  * Show me half of your counters. … Show me half of your page.'

Treating mathematics difficulties seriously

* Identify pupils who are finding mathematics difficult, and provide appropriate intervention.
* Consider whether you need to upgrade your resources and support for pupils with difficulties in mathematics.
* Treat difficulties with mathematics with the same seriousness as you treat difficulties with literacy.
* Demonstrate a belief that difficulties in mathematics, like all other subjects, can be effectively managed by appropriate teaching and sufficient practice.
* Discourage your pupils from 'talking down' their mathematics abilities.
* Look at the vocational needs of older pupils. Relate mathematics teaching to real-life mathematics. Do everything you can to assist pupils to achieve the necessary standard of mathematics to meet their aspirations.

* Challenge stereotypes, such as mathematics being too difficult to master or girls not being good at mathematics.

Making mathematics a positive experience

* Be a good role model. Show positive anticipation and enjoyment of mathematics activities yourself.
* Provide interesting mathematics games, computer activities and puzzles as part of the range of free-choice activities to promote the idea that mathematics can be fun.
* Match the mathematics taught to the pupil's capabilities, so that all pupils enjoy success.

Helping parents to help with mathematics at home

* Encourage parents to involve their children in real-life mathematics. You may like to use Appendix Form 41 'Parent guide to mathematics at home' as a parent information sheet.
* Invite parents into your classroom to observe mathematics lessons in action. This allows parents to see the diversity of activities that form part of understanding mathematics.
* Run a hands-on mathematics session for the parents, so they can try out the mathematics that their child is learning in school.
* Send mathematics work home with clear guidelines, so parents know what is required and how it relates to the development of skills in class.
* Create attractive and interesting mathematics displays in school with so parents are aware of the learning taking place.
* Make a list or create activity boxes of practical mathematics activities covering a wide range of areas. Families can read through the lists or borrow the activity boxes so they can do the activities together at home.
* When you are putting together a show for the parents to watch, include an item that relates to mathematics, such as some amazing mathematics facts or mathematics puzzles along with the songs, readings and other activities.
* Have a wide range of mathematics books that pupils can borrow from the class library and take home.

Encouraging risk taking and exploration in mathematics

* Emphasise that experimenting and exploring are good ways of doing mathematics.
* Show your pupils by example that you often need to make several attempts at finding a solution. Think aloud, so your pupils can hear how you think things through and have several possible ways of doing something.
* Invite pupils to suggest alternative working methods or approaches, presenting the clear message that often several correct solutions are possible. For example:
  * 'Now how are we going to do this? We need to find out how many sheets of paper we have. Any ideas of the best way to count them?'
  * 'We need to leave some space for the big poster that is coming next week. How shall we estimate how much space to leave?'
  * 'We'll need to keep the scores. Any suggestions on how we could do that?'
  * 'Now how could we do this question in our mathematics book? I think there are two or three good ways to do it … maybe more. Any suggestions?'
* Have your pupils ask older pupils and adults to solve a set of problems that you assigned. Ask your pupils to talk about all the different ways that people have used to solve the problem. For example: 'Work out how much water there is in the classroom fish tank', 'Calculate how many people there were at the stadium for the match' or 'Work

out the budget for a family trip'. Your pupils will see that there is often guesswork, approximation and risk-taking involved.

* Make a classroom display to demonstrate the range of ways that different people will tackle the same mathematics task. Following are ways that different people would determine how much water the fish tank holds:
  * Todd's dad would take the water out of the tank in buckets, and he would count how many buckets he used.
  * Tahlia's brother would measure the tank and then work out the volume.
  * Benjamin's mother would look to see if the tank had any writing on it to tell how much it held.
  * Sonja's grandpa would guess it held the same as three cans of oil from the garage, and so that would be about 30 litres.

* Ask pupils to explain how they worked something out. Invite other pupils to describe their methods. As the teacher, you may be able to suggest different ways, too. 'If we are adding 13 + 8, I could count on after 13 for 8 numbers, like this: 14, 15, 16, 17, 18, 19, 20, 21. Or, I could work out that 3 + 8 = 11 and then add 10 to get 21.'

* Look through newspapers and magazines with your pupils, and discuss which figures were probably exact (a sports score, a date) and which were probably estimated (the size of the crowd at the match, the cost of a new airplane).

* Teach pupils to recognise when an approximation is all that is necessary. Practise estimating answers.

* Encourage pupils to estimate before they begin to calculate as a way of checking their final solutions.

Understanding how difficulties occur

* Pupils will often think they have understood when they have not, so avoid saying things such as, 'Everyone okay with that? If you are not sure, then come up to my desk.' Some pupils will not realise they need help!

* Pupils may be self-conscious about having difficulties and feel reluctant to ask for help. Check how well pupils understand by watching them work. Observe whether they are following the correct procedures.

* Avoid asking, 'What don't you understand?' Being able to explain what you do not understand is very difficult. It needs insight into the task or concept to be able to identify what is confusing or unclear.

* Ask a pupil to think aloud when working through a troubling task. Listen to the way the pupil thinks through the problem, and note what procedures are being used. Frequently, you can discover the cause of the problem. You will then have an idea of what to do. Often the pupil is confused with some of the information or rules, or is using an incorrect method to arrive at the answer. 'I said to myself, six take away nine you can't do. So you pretend it's nine take away six, and that's easy.' Or 'If I start with 203, zero is nothing, so it's just 2, 3, and that's 23.'

* Ask the pupil to explain the method used to arrive at the answer, for example:
  * Tell me, what did you do first?'
  * 'What did you say to yourself next?'
  * 'Show me how you used the blocks to work that out.'
  * 'Let me hear you counting that again.'

* Look at the pupil's work to see if you can find any systematic errors in how they work. For instance, what is the pattern in these errors?

      12 + 3 = 14
      11 + 9 = 19
      15 + 4 = 18

The correct answer is one more than the pupil's answer. In this example, it would be a good idea to check how the pupil is working with counters or fingers, if used. Chances are, these pupils are using the first number as the starting point for counting: 12 + 3 = 12, 13, 14

✱ Use tests or independent class assignments, so you can be sure the pupil is doing the work correctly. Look at the errors that occur to find out exactly what the pupil is doing wrong. Obviously, if you find pupils have not mastered the topic you have just taught, provide additional teaching, support and practice.

Using inclusive strategies

✱ Individualise instruction, so all pupils have work they understand.
✱ In any classroom, there will be marked individual differences in pupils' mathematics abilities. It is essential that your classroom programme have a range of levels of instruction to ensure that all pupils are included in a programme that meets their individual needs.
✱ A pupil's difficulty in mathematics could be due to missed schooling or poor teaching at an earlier stage. Keep an open mind about the pupil's capabilities until you have seen their response to good teaching.
✱ A difficulty in one area of mathematics does not mean that the pupil will have difficulties with other areas. For instance, a pupil may have problems with mental computation but be brilliant at problem solving. Allow for flexible grouping according to the type of mathematics activity.
✱ Monitor pupils' progress in mathematics very carefully. Learning mathematics is very easily disrupted by small gaps in understanding. Take particular care to make sure that pupils really have grasped the work they are doing before you introduce new work.
✱ Take into account the different rates of learning in your class. The pupils who understand a topic quickly can move on to the next stage as soon as they are ready. Other pupils who learn more slowly will need a longer period of instruction and a more extended period of consolidation of skills and understanding.
✱ Although your pupils will be working on various levels of difficulty in your mathematics programme, it is usually possible to have the whole class work together on the same topic or area of study – for example, timetables and schedules (see Table 4.2).

Providing plenty of practice

✱ After providing clear instruction and demonstration, have a guided practice session. While pupils work through the task, monitor their performance and prompt them as necessary to help them stay on track.
✱ The development of good mathematics skills is very dependent on practice. Allow enough practice time for all pupils to feel confident applying what you have taught them.
✱ Pupils who find mathematics difficult often make mistakes and work slowly. These pupils are especially at risk of missing out on the practice they really need. Make sure these pupils receive extra practice material, and allow enough time for them to work through all the practice items.
✱ Select similar exercises from several parallel books, and make booklets for intensive practice. This means the pupils will have enough opportunity to practice but will have new activities as they work through the booklet.
✱ Always make sure that pupils who have been absent from school have adequate time for catch-up learning and sufficient practice to enable them to absorb what they missed.
✱ Before introducing a new topic, provide all pupils with a thorough review of previously taught foundation concepts and skills, and provide some practice time. If any pupils

Table 4.2 Differentiating a mathematics activity to suit varying levels of mathematics development

All pupils	General discussion on when and where pupils have seen or used timetables and schedules.
Level 1	Pupils are making a timeline of their daily routines, from getting up to going to bed, including their school schedule.
Level 2	Pupils are reading simple timetables to find departure and arrival times.
Level 3	Pupils are planning trips, using timetables to coordinate several modes of transportation.
Level 4	Pupils are planning trips across different time zones and over the international date line.

do not understand the preliminary work, revise their programme so they have an opportunity to master the prerequisite material before moving to the more difficult levels.

* Use computer mathematics programs for extra practice in basic skills. Programs can be used to reinforce an activity that has been done in class.

Monitoring and supporting

* Make sure pupils understand that the assignments match their level of competence. 'See, this is just like the work you did yesterday, but today you have some different shapes to work with.'
* Arrange for a classmate to be a 'mathematics partner' to provide help when needed.
* Provide appropriate intervention based on pupils' individual needs so they don't have to leave tasks unfinished or incorrect because they did not understand the assignment.
* Use sketches to turn mathematics problems into pictures.
* Provide an example of an almost identical problem alongside the new task.
* Write the steps in the process as part of the worksheet.

Building confidence in mathematics

* Build confidence and understanding by supportive coaching, which provides the pupil with feedback in areas where they are succeeding: 'You are great at getting your ruler right at the beginning of the line.'
* Celebrate what the pupil can achieve, and work on what they have found difficult.
* Suggest that pupils write a note next to items or concepts they do not understand. As you are marking their work, you can see where they knew they had a problem.
* Avoid using worksheets or books that look like 'little kids' stuff'. Select materials that have illustrations and examples that suit the pupil's age and interests. It is just as easy to add up hamburgers or soccer scores as it is to add up toy bears or little ducks!
* Provide a reference sheet with examples of all the previously taught skills. Label all the examples. Also label all the items on the pupil's worksheet, so they can match up the example with the current task. For instance, label an example of *Subtraction with Regrouping*, and also label the new questions on the worksheet *Subtraction with Regrouping*.
* Be sure that a pupil with a reading difficulty can read the mathematics worksheet. Provide extra support if necessary.
* Keep the atmosphere as relaxed as possible. Avoid using timed tests or rushing pupils to finish work.
* Let the pupils select the level of work they feel they can handle.
* Avoid making the pupils give their marks in front of their peers.
* Set up extra, optional mathematics activities to support class work, and allow pupils to determine whether or not they would like to join the group doing them.

Making mathematics relevant

✳ Be creative in the examples you use when teaching mathematics. Relate mathematics to topics such as the environment, social issues, family, sports, art, construction, music, pets, food and so on, so pupils can visualise and relate to the mathematics you are teaching.

✳ Have pupils look for any mathematics-related information in their homes and community: a shopping advertisement, a sports announcement, a label from a container, a postage stamp, etc. Collect the items at school, and then discuss them, create collections and draw out mathematics understanding.

- 'What weight is a regular box of cereal?'
- 'What other things weigh about the same?'
- 'Why is the cereal box so big compared to a packet of cheese that weighs the same?'
- 'How much does it cost to go to the match?'
- 'How much would it cost for everyone in the class to go?'

✳ Create links between mathematics and real-life interests. With mathematics calculation worksheets, talk to the pupils about how the calculations relate to real life: 'Today we are doing this mathematics sheet of multiplication. For 13×12, you could imagine that you were a farmer putting new chicks into their cages. You have 13 cages with 12 chicks in each. Or, maybe you are making muffins, and you have 13 trays with 12 muffins on each. Or, you have 13 bags with 12 marbles in each bag.'

✳ Relate mathematics work to your pupils' individual interests by creating parallel worksheets. The mathematics is exactly the same in each version of the sheet. Sheets can relate to the environment, creative activities, favourite sports, money or whatever interests them. For instance, most basic problems can easily relate to the number of birds in a rain forest, measurements for a craft project, scores in a game, or the balance of a savings account.

✳ Use every opportunity within your classroom to show how mathematics is used over and over again in many different situations that are useful and interesting.

✳ Ask the pupils to talk to their families about how they use mathematics. Make a classroom display of the results.

- Gina's grandmother counts her stitches when she knits
- Teddy's sister gives change in the supermarket
- Sunni's dad measures the wood for the houses he build

✳ If you have a mathematics corner or an area where you keep mathematics materials, use it as often as you can, right across the curriculum.

- 'Jack, could you get the counters from the mathematics shelf to help us keep the score in this game.'
- 'Hey! We can use the mathematics tape measure to measure and see if we can get the new art desk through the door.'
- 'If we use the mathematics blocks, we can figure out how we can all fit in the school bus for our trip.'

✳ All learning is more interesting if it links into everyday interests. Encourage your pupils to keep interesting mathematics information in journals, charts or a database.

- Keep track of your local team's scores
- See how accurate the local weather forecast is
- Develop a database on the pupils. Make a spreadsheet of the information
- Make a timetable of favorite TV shows

✳ Encourage the pupils to think mathematically, and highlight when they have done so.

- 'I liked the way you used mathematics to see if you have written enough for your journal.'

- 'That was good mathematics thinking to get all those things packed away in that box.'
* Suggest activities that involve several areas of the curriculum.
    - 'Write a story. You must include some counting and measuring in the story.'
    - 'Plant several different types of seeds. Make a chart to show how they grow.'
    - 'Make a score sheet for your personal spelling tests. Track your performance for four weeks.'
* Ask your pupils to look around the classroom and challenge each other.
    - 'Find six things with acute angles in the classroom.'
    - 'Find patterns of three.'
    - 'Find examples of symmetry.'
    - 'Find something that has over 1,000 parts.'
    - 'What is the largest written number in the room?'
    - 'Find 20 things that are less than one centimetre long.'
* At the end of each school day, give the pupils a summary of the day's learning. Include not only formal mathematics lessons but any other mathematics that occurred incidentally. 'We did quite a bit of mathematics by working out which pupils are old enough to sign up for the new athletic team.' … 'In designing our class newsletter, we had a lot to fit on the page. All that measuring and trying out the sizes was good mathematics work.'

Pupil has difficulties understanding the number system

Mathematics observation chart: section 2

---

2. Pupil has difficulties in understanding the number system

Pupil makes errors when counting

Pupil makes errors when working with place value

Pupil makes errors in addition and subtraction

Pupil does not understand the relationship between addition and subtraction (e.g., cannot use the missing addend to solve subtraction)

Counting

Remembering a long sequence of numbers can be difficult for many young pupils, or for older pupils with significant developmental disabilities. Counting is a foundation skill, and many pupils with difficulties need explicit teaching of the basics before they can move on to more advanced work.

Just saying the numbers in order is not of any real value. You must be able to apply this in a useful way. You need to be able to:

- recite the numbers and relate them one by one to objects
- match a written number to a spoken word
- stop at the right place in the counting sequence
- count in reverse
- make a decision about what sort of counting to use. When is it better to count by 10s? What if there are so many that you can't count every single one?

Place value

As a very young pupil, you learn that the number 3 refers to three single items. Later you come across the numerals 37 or 3,931 and find out that the 3 in these examples is not three single items at all, but a far larger quantity. Understanding place value is, of course, an absolute foundation of mathematics. The only difference between 109 and 901 is the position of two of the numbers.

Place value is a clever system, because it allows us to use just 10 symbols to represent an infinite range of numbers. However, pupils with learning difficulties often find the system very confusing. Without understanding place value, even basic counting is much more difficult. As an adult, you know the number that comes after 3,729, even though you have never learned to count by rote to that number.

Zero is particularly confusing for some young learners. Usually children learn that zero is nothing and may think that whenever they see a 0, they can ignore it, remove it or pretend it doesn't exist. Although 0 is used to represent nothing, it is also used as a place holder in numbers such as 203 and 190, and as such, cannot be ignored. This is a hard concept for some pupils to handle.

Addition and subtraction of numbers and application of missing addend

Understanding the addition and subtraction of numbers is a fundamental concept that supports later development in mathematics. Once pupils understand that a number can be made up of two or more smaller numbers, they can begin to manipulate that knowledge. If you know that 3 + 4 = 7, then you also know that 4 + 3 = 7. If you know that the number 12 is made up of 4 + 8, then 12 − 4 is a simple matter of deduction that does not require counting.

Understanding halves and doubles is a very useful part of addition and subtraction and can lead to skilled mental computation.

Strategies for building mathematics skills in understanding the number system

Working with counting

* Counting real objects is very important, as well as using counting rhymes, songs and stories. Provide young pupils with plenty of practice counting real things.
* For older pupils who are still learning to count, make sure you frequently count out loud in the classroom as you distribute books, count pupils and organise activities.
* Discourage rapid counting before the pupil can touch count. Some young pupils can recite the number sequence without understanding. It is better to count slowly and clearly.
* Get pupils to notice numbers all around them. 'What is your street number? … What is the number of the house next door or across the street? … How many TV channels do you receive? … How far has the family car travelled?'
* In the classroom, number the desks, chairs, coat hooks, shelves, worksheets, books and any other objects that can consolidate the pupils' awareness of numbers.
* Count objects of different size. Teach that the number 5 is the same, regardless of whether you are counting 5 elephants or 5 ants.
* If pupils find touch counting (touching and counting items one by one) difficult, introduce the easier activity of saying names and touching. Provide pupils with toy items, and ask them to touch and name each one in turn: 'Duck, cat, dog, cat, duck, duck, dog …' You can do the same with coloured dots or shapes. The pupil touches and names the colour: 'Red, blue, blue, yellow, red …'

* The easiest form of counting is to count all items in a set. So start at this level. Provide various objects to count, and encourage accurate touch counting. Gradually build up the number of items the pupil can count, always adding just one more. Do not suddenly shift from counting, say, three items to counting twelve items.
* Counting and stopping at a given number is a more difficult task than just counting everything in a set. Once the pupil can accurately count an entire set, ask them to count out a specific quantity from a larger set. For example, put 25 counters on the desk, and ask the pupil to count out only 12.
* Provide plenty of explicit teaching, relating the link between written numbers and the spoken sequence. Give the pupils number sets written on separate cards. The pupils can put the cards in the correct sequence and count the sequence.
* Always have a clear number line in view in your classroom or on the pupils' desks. Pupils will be able to check the number sequence when they need to.
* For older pupils, provide a number line for their mathematics books. A clearly marked, metric measuring ruler can be used as a reliable number line.
* Encourage pupils to notice the numbering system in books: 'How many pages does this book have?'
* Ask pupils to number every page in their workbooks.
* Show pupils how to use the word count in their computer software when they write and work towards specific word totals.
* Encourage pupils to recognise small quantities without counting. Many pupils with difficulties count each item in any display. Pupils should be able to look at up to five items and know how many there are without counting.
* Counting in reverse is an important skill. Model this type of counting as you check off pupils leaving the room: '28, 27, 26 …'
* Have pupils do 'space take-off' counting, where they count backwards to 'lift off'.
* Use counting in 2s and 10s as you work with the pupils to show them how to vary the way they count.
* Have pupils help with classroom inventory to develop an awareness of different types of counting. Is it important to count every piece of paper, or can the pupils use the knowledge that the paper is packaged with 100 sheets per pack?
* Number the days of the year from 1 to 365, and keep track in your class of where you are in the year, day by day. For example, 'Today is the 96th day of the year.'
* Talk about the position of numbers on a number line: 'Which number comes right after 39? What number comes before 99?'
* Make a number line and omit some of the numbers. Provide the missing numbers to the pupils, and see how quickly they can determine their correct positions.
* Teach estimating skills. Encourage pupils to guess large quantities, and then check their guesswork with some serious counting. Have pupils check how close the estimates are to the actual count.
* Give the pupils two clear jars, partly filled with beads, beans or other small items. Tell them how many beads are in one jar, and ask them to estimate how many in the other. Do the same with beads on a string, grains of rice on a plate and so on.

Working with place value

* Give plenty of counting activities, where items are grouped into 10s and clearly marked. Have boxes, bags and jars and lots of different types of real objects to count, such as paperclips, ribbons, shells, pencils, beads, etc. At first, just count in tens and label your groups: 'We have six bags of shells, so that's 10, 20, 30, 40, 50, 60 shells altogether. We'll put the number 60 on a card on the desk to show how many we have.'
* Put together sealed packets of items in sets of 10, 20, 50 and 100. You also could look in hardware stores for prepackaged small items (such as screws, nails, or hooks), which

often come in 10s, 50s and 100s. Ask the pupils to put together various quantities without opening any of the boxes. This means they have to work without counting one by one. ('Put 250 screws on the table. ... Give me 320 buttons.') The pupils should write the numbers to consolidate their understanding of place value.

* Because pupils cannot 'see' the 10s in a number such as 35, they are often confused and think that they have a 3 and a 5. Show them how the number is built up from the number 30 + 5 by using two layers of cards. (See Figure 4.1.)
* Continue to use the layer system to teach three- and four-digit numbers. (Figure 4.2.)
* Have pupils watch a counter (such as a pedometer or odometer) as the numbers increase, for example, from 49 to 50 or 99 to 100, and talk to the pupils about how the place values change. 'We had nine tens and nine ones, and now we have one hundred.'
* Encourage pupils to navigate through books using the index and page numbers. Use indexes and page numbers as a teaching tool for place value. Ask pupils to say where a certain page number will be found: 'Page 103 will be just after 100 but way before the 200s. ... If I am on page 44 and I want page 85, I have to go forward about 40 pages.'
* Use page numbers and indexes in an informal assessment of the pupils' grasp of place value. When asked to find a page, do they search at random for the number? Can they explain how to look for a particular page?
* For older pupils, have a line that goes up to at least 1,000 with the changes in place value clearly marked.
* Make a collection of whole numbers. Have pupils find and bring in any numbers from any source and write the numbers clearly on strips of paper. Pin the numbers on a board in order of size, rearranging the display as new numbers are introduced. Encourage the pupils to decide where a new number has to be positioned. 'Bobbie has found the

Figure 4.1 Using card layers to build two-digit numbers

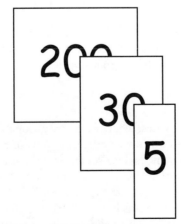

Figure 4.2 Using card layers to build three-digit numbers

number 150 on his lunchbox. Where does it go? That is correct; it comes in between 120 and 275.'

✱ For younger pupils, create a number line 1–100 with numbers missing. Have the pupils fill in the missing numbers.

✱ For older pupils, create a column of numbers in chronological order with some digits missing. Have the pupils fill in the missing numbers.

    2321
    2322
    2*23
    23*4
    232* and so on

Working with addition and subtraction of numbers

✱ Accept that some pupils with learning difficulties will not be able to memorise the number facts. Encourage these pupils to use the number charts. You can copy Appendix Form 12 'Addition chart' and Appendix Form 13 'Subtraction chart' for your pupils.

✱ Teach pupils to use a calculator correctly. Many pupils with learning difficulties struggle endlessly with basic number facts, when the use of a calculator would allow them to succeed with more interesting work.

✱ Have a number of the week, and have pupils really focus on this number. For example, if 5 is the number of the week, some of the following activities may be appropriate.
  • Make patterns of five with pebbles, shells, bricks, cups, pencils or any items available.
  • Photograph or draw your patterns of five.
  • Make more patterns of five with markers, ink stamps or paper shapes.
  • Find patterns of five around you: five fingers, five toes, five petals.
  • How many different ways can you arrange five things?

✱ For pupils who are finding mathematics difficult, *Number of the Week* can be a good exercise right through to large numbers such as 25, 100 or even larger.

✱ Make a class poster of every number that you focus on. This remains posted so that in later weeks, pupils with difficulties can refer to it.

✱ Encourage pupils to recognise number patterns without counting. Hold up various number patterns, and ask the pupils to say how many things they see. (Figure 4.3.)

✱ With the pupils' help, develop a number chart showing all the possible number combinations up to 10. The two forms Appendix Form 12 'Addition chart' and Appendix Form 13 'Subtraction chart' can be photocopied for individual pupils to use.

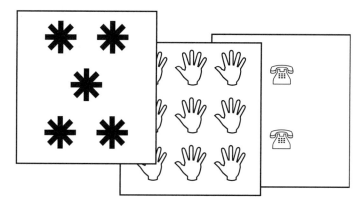

Figure 4.3 Recognising number patterns

* Show pupils how the addition chart can be used to find the answers to subtraction problems. ('If 2 + 5 = 7, then what is 7 – 2?') For pupils with learning difficulties, you may need to demonstrate this with real objects over and over again.

* Play matching games for pupils to practice basic number facts. Write single numbers and symbols (+ – =) on small note cards. Give each pupil about 20 cards. Then write a whole number up on the board. Can the pupils make the number with their cards? For example, if you write 9, pupils can show cards 3 + 3 + 3 or 10 – 1. Once the pupil uses the cards, they are turned over and no longer in play. Continue the game until at least one pupil has discarded all of his cards. This pupil is the winner.

* Count in 3s or 4s or any other number to teach the intervals between numbers. For more able pupils, vary the starting point to make it harder. For example, start from 2 and count in 3s: *2, 5, 8, 11, 14 ...*

* Make doubles of numbers using paint. Fold a piece of paper in half. Use wet paint to make dots on one half only. Immediately fold the paper over so that the wet paint makes an equal number of dots on the other half of the page. Have the pupils build a chart of double number facts: The number 6, when doubled, is 12. ... The number 7, when doubled, is 14.

* Halves are harder to learn than doubles. Teach doubles and halves together: 'The number 11 doubled is 22, so half of 22 is 11.'

* Make a classroom chart of doubles and halves and keep it where pupils can refer to it as they work.

* Teach odd and even numbers. You can show pupils how odd numbers are the numbers that do not have equal halves, so there is always an 'odd one out' when an odd number of things is shared. Use sets of beads or other small items to share between two containers, and record whether you can split the number of items equally or not.

* Ask the pupils to make patterns using odd and even numbers of buttons. What sorts of patterns won't work with an odd number of buttons?

* Make an individual or classroom chart of odd and even numbers, so pupils who do not yet understand the concept can still use the information when needed.

Pupil has difficulties with the four operations

Mathematics observation chart: section 3

---

3. Pupil has difficulties with the four operations

The pupil uses tangible objects to count without real understanding

The pupil has difficulty applying standard algorithms

The pupil makes errors in addition

The pupil makes errors in subtraction

The pupil makes errors in multiplication

The pupil makes errors in division

Using tangible objects to count

Many pupils are confused by counters, chips, blocks and other manipulative materials that are frequently used in school for curriculum support. Pupils often do not realise that these items are supposed to represent real objects and are not ends in themselves. This makes mathematics work abstract and uninteresting. Does it really matter if you have ten counters?

It was only when I started teacher training myself, that I realised those wooden blocks were only meant to stand in for real objects. I don't think we ever thought about it at the time. Didn't we ever wonder why the teacher was so interested in how many blocks we had, day after day?

Many of us sometimes use our fingers to count, or we make tally marks as adults as an aid in calculation. In itself, this is not a problem. However, pupils with learning difficulties may become confused as they use their fingers, or they may scatter tally marks, so the marks are difficult to count accurately.

Understanding algorithms

Pupils frequently find written algorithms difficult to understand, because often they don't understand that what they are seeing when they look at 6 + 5 or 10 − 3 is a coded set of instructions that requires physical or mental action.

Addition

Addition is the easiest of the four operations to understand, because it is very concrete. If you see 6 + 5, then you do have a real 6 and a real 5. It relates directly to earlier work that the pupils should have done on composition and decomposition of numbers.

There is a developmental sequence in the addition methods that pupils use. These methods range from concrete, physical counting through to mental deduction or recall of known facts.

Table 4.3 is part of Appendix Form 15: 'Mathematics checklist: addition (single-digit numbers)'. You may reproduce it and record your observations of individual pupils.

Pupils with learning difficulties may well prefer to stay with the safest, most concrete methods long after their classmates have moved on to more abstract strategies. They may need explicit instruction to learn how to use the more advanced strategies.

The format of the mathematics problem can also challenge pupils. Mathematics problems begin with horizontal positioning, which like reading, is read from left to right.

Table 4.3 Developmental sequence for addition of 4 + 5

Strategy	Pupil's response	✓
Counts each, counts all	1, 2, 3, 4 1, 2, 3, 4, 5 1, 2, 3, 4, 5, 6, 7, 8, 9	
Counts whole group once	1, 2, 3, 4, 5, 6, 7, 8, 9	
Counts on from first number	5, 6, 7, 8, 9	
Counts on from largest number	6, 7, 8, 9	
Works from a known fact	4 + 4 = 8, 8 + 1 = 9	
Retrieves known fact	9	

Later, the mathematics problem changes to vertical positioning, and to solve this problem, the calculation starts on the right and moves towards the left.

---

2 + 3 = 5

In this example, you start on the left and literally read across, taking each symbol in turn.

23
+42

In this example, you start on the right, adding vertically. Then you move one place to the left and add vertically again

---

You can use Appendix Form 19 'Mathematics checklist: addition (two, two-digit numbers, no regrouping)' and Appendix Form 20 'Mathematics checklist: addition (two, two-digit numbers, with regrouping)' to record your pupils' working methods.

Subtraction

Subtraction is much more abstract than addition. Many pupils are tricked by the fact that the numbers they see written on their sheets are not two separate quantities. For example, with 8 – 2 you start with a real 8, but the 2 is already there, 'hidden' within the 8. Many pupils with learning difficulties will get out eight blocks and then another two to start this calculation off.

As with addition, there is a developmental sequence in the way subtraction is handled. Table 4.4 is part of Appendix Form 16 'Mathematics checklist: subtraction (single digits)'. You may reproduce it and record your observations of individual pupils.

Many pupils do not apply existing knowledge of addition facts to subtraction. Instead, they slowly and carefully count to work out number facts that they already 'know' in another form. For example they may know that 3 + 7 = 10, but they work out 10 – 3 by counting. Subtraction is much more effective if the pupil understands the composition and decomposition of numbers.

Vertical subtraction requires the pupil to work from right to left, but also to remember to take the bottom number from the top number. Subtraction with regrouping introduces some further challenges in the process of having to 'borrow' between columns. All of this can really confuse the pupil.

Table 4.4 Developmental sequence for subtraction of 8 – 3

Strategy	Pupil's response	✓
Counts all and then counts back	1, 2, 3, 4, 5, 6, 7, 8 , 7, 6, 5	
Counts back from largest number	7, 6, 5	
Counts up from the lowest number	4, 5, 6, 7, 8	
Works from a known fact	8 – 2 = 6, 6 – 1 = 5	
Retrieves known fact	5	

Table 4.5 Developmental sequence for multiplication of 4 × 5

Strategy	Pupil's response	✓
Counts up in fives	5, 10, 15, 20	
Counts up in fours	4, 8 ,12, 16, 20	
Recites times table	1 × 5 = 5, 2 × 5 = 10, 3 × 5 = 15, 4 × 5 = 20	
Works from a known fact	5 × 5 = 25, 25 – 5 = 20	
Retrieves known fact	20	

You can use Appendix Form 21 'Mathematics checklist: subtraction (two, two-digit numbers, no exchanging)' and Appendix Form 22 'Mathematics checklist: subtraction (two, two-digit numbers, with exchanging)' to record your pupils' working methods.

Multiplication

Multiplication is most easily understood by pupils with learning difficulties as repeated addition. Obviously, this can involve very tedious repeated calculation to arrive at an answer. However, for some pupils this is the best option if they find rote learning difficult.

Often the pupil will assume that all the numbers they see are tangible quantities, so that looking at 4 × 3, they will get out four blocks and then three blocks.

Pupils may also get confused between + and ×, as the two symbols look similar apart from their orientation.

There are several ways of arriving at a multiplication fact such as 4 × 5 = 20. Table 4.5 is part of Appendix Form 17: 'Mathematics checklist: multiplication'. You may photocopy it and record your observations of individual pupils.

Division

Division can be understood as repeated subtraction, although many pupils are comfortable with the 'sharing' concept through real-life experiences. The relationship between multiplication and division is a very important link for the pupils to grasp.

The symbol ÷ can cause confusion, as it is very similar to the subtraction sign.

Table 4.6 is part of Appendix Form 18: 'Mathematics checklist: division'. You may photocopy it and record your observations of individual pupils.

Table 4.6 Developmental sequence for division of 15 ÷ 3

Strategy	Pupil's response	✓
Counts off groups of three	1, 2, 3, 1, 2, 3, 1, 2, 3, 1, 2, 3	
Counts in threes	3, 6, 9, 12, 15 or 15, 12, 9, 6, 3	
Works from a known fact	5 + 5 + 5 = 15 or 3 × 5 = 15	
Retrieves known fact	5	

Strategies for understanding the number system

Using tangible materials

* Encourage all pupils to use concrete supports, such as blocks, charts or fingers, if needed. Remember, many adults still use their fingers to count or calculate!
* Provide pupils with a range of interesting materials, such as shells, buttons, small toys, pebbles and coloured papers for support in mathematics work.
* Continue to use familiar counting aids, such as Cuisenaire rods and Unifix cubes, from one school year to the next, so pupils have continuity of support and learning materials.
* For older pupils, provide more discreet forms of support, such as a ruler or number line, which can be used for counting, or a printed 'abacus' for support with addition. You can copy Appendix Form 11: 'Counting chart'.
* Make your teaching explicit and clear for those pupils who have difficulty. Model the task. Provide a practical demonstration and a verbal commentary. Invite the pupils to participate to hold their interest. Aim to have pupils contribute about 50 per cent of the thinking and action.

  'Now let me see. What do I have to do? Yes, I have to do some adding. We have a 6 and a 3. So let's get out the blocks. Can you do that?'

  'Straighten the blocks, so they are easy to count. Can you handle the counting? That's looking good. Now can you write that number down?'
* Make sure that your pupils understand that the counters, blocks, etc., used in class are simply convenient substitutes for real objects. 'It would be very hard to count the pigs in the farmyard. Let's pretend these blocks are the pigs. Now see how easy it is to count them? They don't run away like real pigs!'
* Use concrete classroom situations that occur outside of the mathematics lesson. 'We have eight pupils running, six swimming, and five at music class. Take out the blocks, and figure out how many pupils are at activities.'
* If pupils use fingers to count, watch to make sure they are using them correctly. For instance, some will double count the same finger or always call their thumb 'number 1'.
* If pupils use tally marks, check to see that they are arranging them neatly, so they can count them accurately. Encourage older pupils to tally in groups of 10 to make counting easier.
* Some pupils will make a fresh set of tally marks for every calculation. This takes up a lot of time. Provide a copy of Appendix Form 11: 'Counting chart', so pupils do not need to constantly draw and count their tally marks. Teach the pupils how to use this counting chart.

Understanding algorithms

* Be sure that pupils are confident with the number system and have had the experience of composition and decomposition of numbers before you introduce formal recording of algorithms.
* Teach the concept and the sign of equivalence (=) as a starting point. Have the pupils match up pairs of cards and use the equal sign (=) to show equivalence. (Figure 4.4.)
* Make sure your pupils understand that the symbols +, −, × and ÷ are codes for action. Every time they see one of these signs, they have to do something, either physically or mentally.
* Explain to the pupils that each of these signs has several names. For example, 'We call this symbol (+) add or plus. ... We call this symbol (−) minus, take away or subtract.'
* Make a classroom chart of the symbols and the words that can be used to describe their functions.

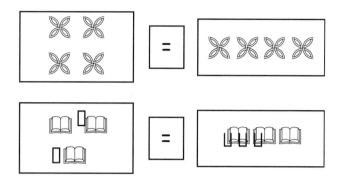

Figure 4.4 Matching up equivalent picture cards

✱   As each symbol is introduced, provide pupils with practical activities, where they have to physically add, subtract, multiply or divide.
    6 + 3: The pupils may get six books and then another three books.
    12 – 5: The pupils may lay 12 counters on their desks and then hide five counters.
✱   Have one pupil manipulate some objects, such as placing six pencils on the table and then adding two more. Have the other pupils write down the algorithm for what happened: 6 + 2 = 8.
✱   Teach the pupils that the first number they see in an algorithm is the number (a real quantity) where they need to start. 'I have to start with 12.'
✱   Teach the pupils that the symbol and the number that follows the symbol describe the 'job' that has to be done. Ask pupils to circle the symbol and the number and tell you what job must be done. 'I have to take away 7. … I have to divide it into 3. … I have to multiply it by 4.' (Figure 4.5.)
✱   When working with a vertical calculation, teach the pupil to recognise that the number at the top is the starting point and the sign and the number at the bottom is the job to be done. (Figure 4.6)

Understanding addition

✱   Observe the pupils to see which methods they are using for addition. Appendix Form 15: 'Mathematics checklist: addition' may be used to document the strategies a pupil uses and any observations. Look at the list of methods, and see if it is possible to introduce the pupil to a more advanced level.
✱   Teach addition facts in class. Take a few minutes each day to rehearse quick recall of number facts.
✱   Provide pupils with a copy of Appendix Form 12: 'Addition chart'.
✱   For pupils with persistent difficulties with addition, allow the use of a calculator in place of mental computation.

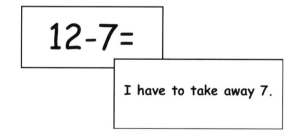

Figure 4.5 Reading the symbol as the 'job' to be done

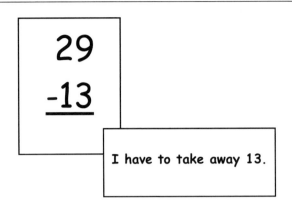

Figure 4.6 Reading the 'job' in a vertical calculation

* Many pupils with learning difficulties always use a concrete counting method, even when they know some number facts. Have the pupils complete an addition facts worksheet and use a highlighter to highlight the addition facts they know for memory. Encourage the pupils to work through the sheet, simply entering the numbers in the places they have highlighted.

* Teach the pupils 'counting on' to replace the 'counting all' method. Tell the pupils, 'We are going to do some counting. I am going to start, and then when I stop, you are going to continue on with the counting.' For example, you count 'one, two, three, four, five' and the pupil picks up 'six seven, eight, nine, ten'.

* For a group of pupils, place a pile of buttons in the middle of the table. Each pupil takes a handful of buttons. The counting goes around the table, with each pupil counting on from the previous total, until they have determined the total number of buttons. For example, the first pupil counts 'one, two, three', the next pupil continues 'four, five, six, seven, eight, nine', and so on, until all the buttons have been counted.

* Prepare some picture cards with various items. Write the number of items on each card. Give each pupil two cards, and ask the pupil to work out the total, by saying only the number on the first card and then counting the rest of the items on the second card one by one. So, for example, the pupil will look at the first card and say 'six' and then continue by counting the rest of the items on the second card: 'seven, eight, nine, ten'.

* Encourage the pupils to use the 'trick' of counting on from the largest number to make the task easier.

* Give the pupils a sheet of simple addition and ask them to underline the largest number in each algorithm. Then provide supervised practice with counting on from that number. They may need to make tally marks for the smaller number to assist with counting on. (Figure 4. 7.)

* Use Appendix Form 11: 'Counting chart' to support pupils who need something tangible to count.

* Teach pupils to look for known addition facts and to work from there.
    If 6 + 6 =12, then 6 + 7 =
    If 5 + 5 =10, then 5 + 4 =

* Before introducing the concept of vertical addition, thoroughly review place value, as pupils may have forgotten the basics. In particular, practice making sets of 10. For example, have the pupils count out beads into groups of 10 and record the number: 'Three groups of 10 and four left over is 34'.

* Use concrete materials to support early work on vertical addition with regrouping.

$$\underline{6} + 4 =$$
$$_{||||}$$

$$4 + \underline{7} =$$
$$_{||||}$$

$$6 + \underline{8} =$$
$$_{||||||}$$

$$\underline{7} + 3 =$$
$$_{|||}$$

Figure 4.7 Using tally marks for 'counting on'

Understanding subtraction

✱ Observe the pupils and see which subtraction methods they are using. Appendix Form 21: 'Mathematics checklist: subtraction' can be used to note the strategies a pupil uses and your observations. Look at the list of methods, and see if it is possible to introduce the pupil to a more advanced level.

✱ Teach (or re-teach) how to interpret written algorithms: 'Start with the first number. The sign and the next number tell you what to do'.

✱ Teach subtraction facts in your class. Take a few minutes each day to review quick recall of number facts.

✱ Do not introduce subtraction until your pupils are confident with the concept of composition and decomposition of numbers (see previous section). Teach number facts in clusters of four related facts. For example:

✱ $4 + 5 = 9$ $5 + 4 = 9$ $9 - 4 = 5$ $9 - 5 = 4$

✱ Provide pupils with a copy of Appendix Form 13: 'Subtraction chart'.

✱ For pupils with persistent difficulties with subtraction, allow use of a calculator in place of mental computation.

✱ Teach pupils to think about differences between numbers to aid in subtraction. Prepare cards with one pair of numbers. The pupils look at the differences between the two numbers and sort the cards into piles: 'The numbers on these cards all have a difference of 3. This pile has numbers with a difference of 5.' (Figure 4.8.)

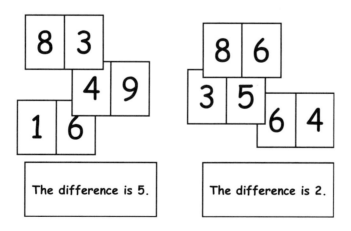

Figure 4.8 Grouping cards with the same difference

✳ Provide pupils with structured worksheets, where they are encouraged to use reason (not count) to arrive at the answer.

If 9 – 6 = 3, then 9 – 5 =

Understanding multiplication

✳ Observe the pupils and see which multiplication methods they are using. Appendix Form 17: 'Mathematics checklist: multiplication' can be used to note the strategies a pupil uses and your observations. Look at the list of methods, and see if it is possible to introduce the pupil to a more advanced level.

✳ Familiarise your pupils with the meaning of the symbol × by making simple instruction cards for them to follow.

Jump × 4.

Draw 5 dogs × 2.

Show me 8 counters × 3.

✳ For pupils who find it difficult to sort out the difference between the symbols + and ×, teach them that × is like + 'rolling along.' Pupils can often relate the idea of addition 'rolling along' to the repeated addition needed for multiplication. The sign tells them how many times the addition has to be repeated, or 'rolled'.

✳ Have the pupils create their own charts of multiplication facts. Start with a small chart, for example a grid of 5 × 5. Then introduce larger charts as the pupils gain competence.

✳ If pupils are ready to learn their multiplications tables, encourage them to recite the whole number fact: 1 × 2 = 2, 2 × 2 = 4, 2 × 3 = 6 ... and discourage simply counting up: 2, 4, 6, 8, ... The counting up method is of little value in real-life situations when immediate access to the information is needed.

✳ Show the pupils how answers are repeated. If you learn 5 × 6, you already know 6 × 5. So once the pupil has learned some of the tables, they already know part of the other tables. For example, once the pupils have learned the 1, 2 and 3 times tables, they know 51 of the 100 facts from the table below! By the time the pupil learns the 8 times table, they only have three new facts to learn (8 × 8, 8 × 9 and 8 × 10).

Appendix Form 14: 'Multiplication chart' which shows multiplication to 100 may be photocopied from the Appendix.

✳ Give pupils regular practice reviewing the times tables, so the response becomes automatic.

✳ Give pupils a multiplication chart with some numbers missing. How quickly can they fill in the empty squares? (Figure 4.9.)

✳ Play a form of 'mathematics bingo.' Each pupil creates a card with 10 numbers on it. (Figure 4.10.)

The caller has the numbers 1–10 written on separate cards. There are at least eight cards for each number, making a minimum of 80 cards in total, The cards are shuffled. The caller selects the top two cards, and the numbers are called out as a multiplication problem, such as 6 × 3. The pupils look for the product on their cards, and if they have the correct answer (in this case 18), a counter is placed over the number. The first pupil to get every number covered with a counter wins the game.

✳ Learning to recite tables by heart is frustratingly difficult for some pupils. Allow these pupils to use Appendix Form 14: 'Multiplication chart' or a calculator to compensate for memory difficulties.

Understanding division

✳ Observe the pupils and see which division methods they are using. Appendix Form 18: 'Mathematics checklist: division' can be used to note the strategies a pupil uses and

	1	2	3	4	5	6	7	8	9	10
1	1		3		5		7		9	
2		4		8		12	14	16		20
3	3	6	9	12	15		21		27	
4		8		16		24		32		40
5	5		15		25	30	35		45	
6		12		24		36		48	54	60
7	7		21		35		49		63	70
8		16		32		48		64		80
9	9		27		45		63		81	
10	10	20		40		60		80		100

Figure 4.9 Completing the multiplication squares

	12	36		18
8	27		16	54
	42	55	21	

Figure 4.10 Mathematics bingo cards

your observations. Look at the list of methods, and see if it is possible to introduce the pupil to a more advanced level.

* Only introduce division when you are certain that the pupils understand composition and decomposition of numbers and multiplication. Show how division is only an extension of decomposition. A number can be decomposed into several smaller numbers of equal value, with or without a remainder.

* Give explicit instruction about the relationship between multiplication and division, and encourage the pupils to use existing multiplication knowledge to solve division problems.

    If $8 \times 4 = 32$, then $32 \div 4 =$

* Provide real materials, such as a box of biscuits, and show how the biscuits can be divided into equal portions. 'If we give each person three biscuits, how many people can we serve? … If we share these biscuits between the six of us, how many biscuits will each person get?'

✳ Teach the ÷ symbol as a special kind of subtraction, where you can keep subtracting until there is nothing left.

✳ Show the pupils how division relates to multiplication by using the Appendix Form 14: 'Multiplication chart'.

✳ Make sets of division and multiplication facts. Ask the pupils to match up each division fact with its corresponding multiplication fact.

Pupil has difficulties with recall

Mathematics observation sheet: section 4

---

4. Pupil has difficulties with recall

Pupil relies on calculator for basic number facts every time they are needed

Pupil makes errors when saying multiplication tables

Pupil forgets algorithms

Pupil does not solve mathematics problems mentally

Many pupils have difficulties with memory. Perhaps they understand the concepts but find it hard to remember the detailed facts. It is important for teachers to determine which pupils fail to provide correct answers because of general difficulties and which pupils fail only because of memory problems.

Memory difficulties alone should not be used as an excuse to hold back otherwise capable mathematics pupils.

Strategies for managing difficulties with recall in mathematics

✳ Do not assess a pupil's mathematics capabilities purely on the ability to recall number facts.

✳ Provide as many reference charts as possible around the classroom and in the pupil's personal learning resources to help them remember number facts.

✳ Make practice of number facts a part of your daily classroom routine.

✳ Computer mathematics games are infinitely patient teachers and may help some pupils learn mathematics facts.

✳ Do not hold a pupil back in mathematics because of memory difficulties, if the difficulties can be overcome with the use of a calculator and/or number charts.

✳ When reciting multiplication tables, some pupils get 'lost' in the sequence. Provide a card with the sequence written down (without the answers), so the pupils can keep their place as they work on their times tables.

✳ Some pupils are able to calculate but not recall. Allow these pupils to calculate the facts that others can remember. If it is a slow process, allow the pupil to use a calculator as an important learning aid.

✳ Pupils with memory difficulties often find mental mathematics very difficult. They forget the question before they have had time to figure out the answer. Provide a written version of the test for the pupils to look at while they mentally figure out the answer to the problem.

✳ For tests that are given orally, often the rate of the questions is too fast for some pupils to mentally process the answers. Ask an adult to give the test individually, so the pace can be adjusted.

✳ Put mental arithmetic tests onto audiotapes, so pupils can work at their own pace and listen to questions several times over.

* Create a reference book of working methods. Write down a step-by-step description of the process to complete a problem, and provide a completed example to demonstrate the process.
* Have pupils keep a personal log of the number facts that they know and add to it as more facts are learned.

Pupil has difficulties with mathematics problems

Mathematics observation chart: section 5

---

5. Pupil has difficulties with mathematics problems

Pupil can solve basic mathematics facts but makes errors when choosing which operation to use in a word problem

Pupil gets confused about what method to use to solve a word problem

---

Some pupils do well when they have a set of numbers in front of them, but once the mathematics problem is changed to a written story problem, they find the work challenging. Maybe the pupil panics at something that looks unfamiliar, or perhaps the pupil finds it difficult to turn a sentence into a mathematics problem.

Sometimes the difficulty is caused by the fact that mathematics has been taught as an abstract process using written numbers, and therefore the pupils are not used to linking mathematics with real, everyday situations.

Strategies for working with mathematics problems

* When teaching any mathematics process, always use practical, real-life examples so the pupils understand that the mathematics they are learning is used in everyday situations.
* Encourage pupils to use blocks, counters, tally marks or the like to represent a word problem: 'A farmer had six sheep, so let's get six blocks and pretend they are sheep. Okay, now what happened next? The farmer went to market and sold four of the sheep … so we can move the blocks along to the market and take four away, because they are sold. Now the farmer bought 10 new sheep, so we get 10 new pretend sheep.'
* Have pupils draw simple sketches of the mathematics problem as an aid to visualising what they have to do.
* Teach pupils to pick out key words that provide a clue about the operation(s) that will be used. Words such as *more, as well, together, bought* and *found* are usually associated with addition; words such as *gave away, lost* and *left* usually suggest subtraction and so on.
* Provide pupils with two very similar word problems – one that shows a completed example and one for the pupil to complete. Explain how the first word problem was solved, and ask pupils to model their reasoning for the second word problem based on the example.

Pupil has difficulties with spatial reasoning

Mathematics observation chart: section 6

---

6. Pupil has difficulties with spatial reasoning

Pupil does not use concrete mathematics materials effectively

Pupil's written numbers and symbols are untidy

Pupil's mathematics work is unorganised and difficult to follow

Pupil expresses confusion when working with spatial mathematics skills

---

While we often think of mathematics as connected with numbers and numerical operations, many types of mathematics depend on spatial awareness and problem solving.

Pupils with poor spatial skills may have problems in laying their work out neatly, or they may find it hard to use concrete counting materials accurately. For instance, they may use tally marks for counting but arrange the marks in a scattered pattern so that counting is difficult.

Some areas of the mathematics curriculum, such as symmetry, tessellation (mosaics) and geometry, deal directly with spatial skills, and this may challenge some pupils.

Strategies for working with spatial reasoning in mathematics

* Show pupils how to lay out tally marks or counters neatly, in tidy columns or rows. For older pupils, encourage grouping in 10s to make counting easier.
* Provide explicit teaching and extra practice for writing numerals and symbols for pupils who find it difficult. Give a verbal commentary on figure formation, so the pupils have a script to guide them. 'Let's write the number 2. Start at the top and swing out, then swing in and then straight across the bottom.' Left-handed pupils will swing in first and then out.
* Allow pupils to use Appendix Form 11: 'Counting chart' if they have trouble with setting out their own tally marks.
* Use graph paper to help organise the layout.
* Lined paper on its side can help older pupils keep columns straight.
* Use a calculator with a printout to help pupils who have difficulty recording their work neatly.
* Have pupils verbalise the geometric shapes and problems. This may help the pupils to interpret what they see. 'It's like a square, but the bottom has been pulled out wider than the top, so there are still four lines. The top line is shorter than the bottom line, and the lines on the sides slope outwards.'
* Avoid having pupils copy mathematics problems from the board before they can begin the assignment. Instead, provide handouts, so they can start work right away.
* Visually crowded worksheets can overwhelm and confuse. Provide clear and concise layouts with teacher created materials.

Pupil has advanced skills in mathematics

Mathematics observation chart: section 7

---

7. Pupil has advanced skills in mathematics

Pupil demonstrates advanced mathematical thinking

Pupil finds standard class work too easy. Can handle more difficult work

Pupil expresses an interest in mathematics and seeks out interesting mathematics challenges

Pupil makes negative statements about class mathematics

Some pupils are very talented in mathematics. They are capable of advanced mathematical thinking in comparison to their age group. Such pupils may seek out mathematical challenges and thrive in an environment where they are able to tackle complex and engaging mathematics work.

However, these pupils may 'hate' mathematics if they find the class work too easy and boring. With a natural aptitude in mathematics, these pupils will have mastered the basic concepts very quickly. They will not need the same amount of practice and will be able to progress quickly through the mathematics programme. If they must follow the same mathematics programme as other pupils, they may become bored. Bright pupils are often unwilling to work through tedious work to earn the right to more interesting and appropriately challenging work.

Strategies for developing advanced mathematics skills

Individualising instruction

✳ Individualise instruction to include pupils with high mathematics ability. Bright mathematics pupils need a curriculum that matches their ability level, so they are stimulated and challenged.

✳ Assess these pupils regularly to identify their mathematics skills.

✳ Bright mathematics pupils may be more than one or two year levels ahead of their peers so make sure that you assess them in a way that shows the upper extent of their abilities.

✳ Advanced pupils generally need a lot less practice in mathematics. Modify the programme to allow these pupils to shortcut the practice phase of learning, if they have clearly mastered the topic or skill.

✳ Look for mathematics activities that provide the pupils with extra challenges in the application and interpretation of mathematics. For instance, ask the pupils to each devise a budget for a school trip. Provide them with brochures and price lists required for the task. Ask the pupils to compare their various approaches and solutions. 'How can the difference in final costs be explained? How could the trip be made as inexpensive as possible?'

✳ Encourage the pupils to identify the patterns in the work they are doing and use those patterns in their work. 'This one is just double the one I did before.'"

✳ Pupils may be able to draw some conclusions from the work they have done. 'None of my answers are over 100 because. ... All of these are right angles because ...'.

✳ Mathematics challenges do not always have to involve more advanced concepts or techniques. Applying and interacting with basic mathematics in innovative ways can also engage the bright pupil's interest and extend learning. These activities can involve other areas of the curriculum. For example:
  • a project related to an environmental issue involving graphs and statistics
  • a practical construction task involving mathematics in the design and evaluation
  • a school trip where the pupil manages the time table, cost and so on
  • evaluation of a classroom plan, such as rearranging the furniture.

Allowing the pupil to skip basics they can already do

✳ Be careful to avoid simply giving the bright mathematics pupil more of the same. For instance, adding up five-digit numbers is really no more challenging and engaging than adding up two-digit numbers for the bright pupil.

✳ Do not expect bright mathematics pupils to prove they can do easy work. Most likely, they will be bored and perform poorly if they have to do work that is uninteresting and does not challenge them.

✳ Many pupils with high mathematics ability cannot show their work or the process of basic arithmetic, because they simply 'know' the answer without working it out. 'I know that 72 is half of 144, it's just sort of in my head.' Observe carefully how the pupil arrives at answers. Require work to be shown only when the pupil performs obvious calculations or does not arrive at the correct answer.

Placing the pupil in a stimulating mathematics environment

✶ Consider placing the bright mathematics pupil in an upper grade level for mathematics, or alternatively, create an accelerated mathematics group in your class or school.

✶ Develop a mathematics club or mathematics interest group, where capable pupils can enjoy mathematics-related activities as part of their free choice time.

✶ If possible, find an older pupil or adult to mentor pupils of exceptional mathematics ability, to encourage mathematics talk and exploration.

✶ Watch for national or international mathematics competitions that your capable mathematics pupils could enter.

Concluding Chapter 4

In this chapter, you have seen that mathematics has a language of its own and, like reading, can present a variety of challenges to the learner. Pupils in one class can range from those who struggle with mathematics those who excel. What is very confusing to one pupil may be perfectly clear to another, and neither can explain why. The strategies presented here provide ways to adjust the levels of learning mathematics in the classroom and make it engaging with games, charts, physical objects and 'tricks of the trade', while emphasising its relevancy to the pupils' interests and everyday lives. Using these tips and strategies will encourage all pupils to advance their skills and feel included in the world of mathematics.

Chapter 5

Concentration and organisaton

Introduction

Have you ever stood in front of your class, ready to teach and waiting, waiting, waiting for one last pupil to settle down? Have you ever had to go over the same thing again and again because some pupils were not concentrating? Have you ever had to spend time helping a pupil search for a missing assignment sheet or an essential piece of material?

Your answer is almost certainly a very loud 'YES!' to these three questions.

Poor concentration and organisation contribute to frustration and wasted time for the teacher, the class and the individual pupil. In some classes, a significant percentage of time may be spent helping pupils who have difficulties in concentration and organisation.

The ability to concentrate and to be well organised is linked to the overall development of the child. We would not expect a 5-year-old to be able to concentrate or be organised in the same way as a 10-year-old. However, there are also wide individual differences. Indeed, we all know adults who are poorly organised, or who find it really difficult to concentrate for any length of time!

Pupils with concentration difficulties may be just as intelligent and motivated as other pupils. But they may find it genuinely difficult to pay attention and sustain concentration. As a result, they may be seriously disadvantaged and unable to achieve their learning goals, simply because they find it difficult to connect with the classroom programme.

Similarly, the 'executive' skills of thinking ahead, planning, organising, coordinating and prioritising tasks may be real challenges for some pupils. They may leave work until the last minute, lose important papers or equipment and fail to manage their time efficiently. Poor school achievements may be the result of poor organisation rather than lack of ability or low motivation.

In an inclusive classroom, problems with concentration and organisation need to be addressed by a range of strategies.

The section headings in this chapter follow the structure of Appendix Form 4: 'Concentration and organisation observation chart'.

The concentration and organisation observation chart may be photocopied and used to informally assess and record difficulties for individual pupils. The concentration and organisation observation chart is divided into four sections, each focusing on a specific area. As you assess individuals, specific patterns of difficulty may emerge. The sections in the chart will provide a direct link between the recorded concentration and organisation observation chart and the corresponding sections in this chapter that provide strategies to help the pupil in those specific area(s) of need. The four sections of the chart have also been reproduced within the main text of this chapter.

If you are interested in using the strategies without completing an informal assessment of the pupil, the sections will easily guide you through the chapter and provide a quick, easy reference tool for specific strategies. This will enable you to select from the intervention strategies, modifications and adaptations listed to help individuals and small groups of pupils.

The following forms from the Appendix are referred to in this chapter:

Appendix Form 37: 'Pupil reward cards'
Appendix Form 34: 'Pupil plan for getting organised '
Appendix Form 32: 'Pupil priorities chart'
Appendix Form 31: 'Pupil work planner'
Appendix Form 4:   'Concentration and organisation observation chart'.

Pupil is physically restless

Concentration and organisation chart: section 1

---

1. Pupil is physically restless

Pupil is often active and has a very high energy level

Pupil fidgets and moves around even when asked to sit still

Pupil often touches and fiddles with things

Pupil is often loud and hard to quiet down

We all know that physical activity is essential for the healthy development of children and young people. Today, many youngsters do not get enough natural, physical activity outside of school. Perhaps they live in an urban environment where safe, open places to play are limited. Perhaps they like to stay indoors and watch television, play electronic games and so forth. Or, parents may prefer to drive pupils to school instead of having their children walk or ride a bike.

The increasing problem of childhood obesity is obviously linked to the lack of normal, healthy activity. Another unwanted side effect of limited opportunities for physical activity is the way in which some pupils need to 'let off steam' inappropriately in the classroom or playground.

However, even when there are adequate opportunities for physical exercise, some pupils have an abundance of energy that seems inexhaustible. They never seem to get tired and are always moving, often boisterous and usually in a full-speed mode.

One real difficulty for restless pupils is that often they really don't know what it feels like to be still and less active. For these pupils, their restless, active, busy state is what feels absolutely normal. Sometimes, they will indignantly deny they are restless, even when they have been touching, pushing and moving around the entire time. ('But I wasn't fidgeting – I was sitting still.')

'They were always telling me to sit still, but I really thought they were just giving me a hard time. Then one day I saw myself in a home movie of my cousin's wedding, and I can tell you I was really shocked. All the other kids were sitting watching the ceremony, but not me! I was under the chair, then standing up, sitting down, looking all around, pulling weird faces, trying to talk to my Mum, undoing my shirt buttons. …'

Everyone has a need for incoming sensation through the senses of touch, smell, taste, hearing, awareness of body sensation and position (proprioception) and vision. Indeed one of the most powerful forms of torture is sensory deprivation, where humans are deprived of incoming sensations.

We all vary in the amount of sensory stimulation needed to maintain a comfortable level. If you do not believe this, take a look around at the next teachers' meeting and see how many of your colleagues need to create some personal sensory input by fiddling with paper clips, doodling, tapping their pens and so on!

Pupils, too, may need a high level of physical sensation to maintain their sensory comfort zones. This need for sensory input may result in them swinging back on their chairs, flicking their pens, rolling bits of paper or a multitude of other, often irritating, mannerisms.

> It's weird, but if I have to keep very still and not touch anything, my fingers tingle and I don't know what to do with them. It's not a good feeling, like something is really wrong with my hands. As soon as I can touch something, say a paper clip, the tingling in my fingers stops and I feel OK again.

There also are pupils who have a real need for physical contact with others. They will push and shove, wrestle, hug and generally create opportunities to touch other people. Standing in a line can be real trouble for these youngsters. They just cannot resist pulling on the person in front, backing into the person behind them and generally creating a disturbance.

Have you noticed how some pupils cannot sit still on the floor? They lean back on their arms, stick their legs out and constantly move around. The reason for this may be that these pupils lack good muscle control of the upper body. Without this muscle control, it is very difficult to maintain a steady, balanced posture when seated on the floor.

Strategies for managing physical restlessness

Providing opportunity for physical activity

* Recognise that young pupils, in particular, may need to be physically active most of the day.
* Allow for the fact that some pupils (and adults) need frequent physical activity.
* Encourage parents to involve their children in daily physical activities, such as walking to school, playing a sport or playing outside in the neighborhood instead of watching TV or sitting in front of the computer.
* Make sure that all pupils have plenty of opportunities for healthy, physical activity. Some pupils may need intense, vigorous physical activity to let off steam.
* Provide restless pupils with legitimate reasons to get up from their seats. Have pupils bring work up to your desk, or send them on errands to other classrooms.
* If possible, arrange for some physical activities to be in a natural environment, such as a park or playing field, rather than in a building. This may be more likely to meet the pupil's need for large, open surroundings and uninhibited movement.
* Encourage physically active pupils to take up a sport where energy and stamina are assets.
* Depending on your locality, encourage parents to get the pupils to walk or cycle to school instead of being driven.
* If parents are concerned about safety when pupils walk to school alone, encourage parents to set up a 'walking train'. One parent sets off at the far end of the route, adding other pupils along the way. The pupils all walk to school together under the supervision of the parent. Another parent along the way may be able to relieve the first parent, if the distance warrants it.
* Build physical activity into your daily classroom routine.

Managing physical restlessness

* Some physical therapists use a form of deep massage to deal with pupils' high need for sensory input. Ask specialists in your school about this.

* Tolerate pupils' physical restlessness, if it is not doing any harm.
* Provide restless pupils with items such as a squishy ball, piece of play dough or soft eraser to fidget with to meet their needs for physical sensation.
* Provide pupils with good seating of a suitable height and with good back support.
* If pupils are restless sitting on the floor, allow them to sit on chairs or bean bags instead.
* Provide restless pupils with special cushions to sit on, designed to allow for movement and restlessness.
* Seat the pupil in a position on the floor where there is room to move without disturbing other pupils.
* Ask a physical therapist for advice for any pupil who has difficulties sitting on the floor. The therapist may be able to provide the pupil with exercises to strengthen upper-body muscle control.
* In situations where the class usually lines up and the restless pupil causes a disturbance, try allowing the class to move in informal groups to see if it works better.
* When it is essential that pupils sit still and remain quiet, provide clear instructions about what is required. Tell them how long they will need to maintain tight control on their restlessness.
* Do not require pupils to stay physically still for long periods of time, as it is physically impossible for some to comply.
* Encourage the pupils to keep their desks clear of loose items that they will want to touch.
* Allow for some 'wind down' time between energetic activity and quiet working time.

Introducing more settled behavior

* Encourage the pupils to monitor their own activity levels. Many are unaware of how restless they are. Seat the pupil near a mirror or reflective window. This will help some pupils become aware of their own restlessness.
* Get the pupils to use a mirror to see what they look like when they are still. Get them to focus on what it feels like to be physically settled and calm. Some pupils may not be able to tell the difference without the visual feedback.
* Have quiet, calming experiences in your classroom to settle pupils and help them learn how to vary their activity levels.
* Speak and move quietly and calmly yourself. Loud, excitable adults tend to increase restless behavior in pupils.
* Ask parents to enroll their child in junior yoga or tai chi classes. This will help pupils to experience the feeling of body calmness.
* Have the pupil try out various ways of talking, such as quiet, loud, slow and fast talk. Use a video or audio recorder to provide feedback. Encourage the pupil to recognise the different styles of talking, and select the styles to be used in a given situation, such as in the classroom or on the playground.
* Use drama to provide the pupils with experience of what it feels like to have a different activity level. Ask a restless pupil to play the role of a character who is quiet, restrained and calm. You can sometimes use this as a prompt for behavior in the future by reminding the pupil of the character: 'Remember what a great job you did being the palace guard? I'd like you to act like the guard again please, Ben.'
* Talk to the pupils about the characters of various animals: the active monkey, the scurrying ants, the calm, slow-moving tortoise, the watchful owl, etc. Create stereotypes for various styles of behaviour, put posters up in your class and use these visual prompts to remind pupils of what style of behaviour you desire at the moment: 'Think "owl" please, John. Watch and listen carefully.'

Pupil is impulsive and impatient

Concentration and organisation observation chart: section 2

---

2. Pupil is impulsive and impatient

Pupil acts before thinking

Pupil calls out in class

Pupil 'forgets' rules and continues to do the wrong thing

Pupil rushes through school work and makes silly mistakes

Pupil interrupts when others are speaking

Pupil pushes in or becomes frustrated when having to wait for turn

Pupil gets restless and frustrated when having to wait

Pupil often seems to be in a rush

Pupil complains if a task or game takes too long

Impulsive, impatient pupils may often get into trouble. They know the rules, and they know the likely punishments perfectly well, but the trouble is, they don't stop and think before they act.

> I just reacted so quickly that it was all over in a second. It was only later that I thought, 'Oh no! That was against the rules, and the last time I did that I was in big trouble'.

When a pupil has behaved inappropriately, there is usually no sensible answer to the question 'Why did you do that?' The behaviour was so impulsive that it wasn't thought through. The pupil will often feel obliged to say something, making an excuse or blaming others to try to explain the impulsive behaviour.

Impulsive pupils may often have a very poor sense of time. A few seconds feels like hours, and an hour seems like an eternity! They really find it hard to wait their turn or hold back until there is an opportunity to speak. They may forget what they were going to say unless they say it right away.

Impulsive, impatient pupils often make a lot of careless mistakes with their schoolwork. They quickly begin without checking what they are supposed to do, they start before they have a plan and finish as fast as they can. It is unlikely that these pupils will stop and check their work before handing it in.

Strategies for managing impulsivity and impatience

Creating a calm, thoughtful atmosphere in your class

* Be clear and methodical in your own teaching.
* Plan every lesson well ahead so that you know exactly you are doing.
* Organise equipment ahead of time to avoid the last-minute panic of trying to find what is needed.
* Try not to rush pupils. Give plenty of time for tasks to be done properly.
* Impose thinking time before getting pupils to start a task: 'Everyone, take two minutes to look over this assignment. Don't pick up your pencils yet; just look at the paper and think about what you have to do.'
* Impose checking time at the end of the task: 'Everyone, take two minutes to look through your work. Check that you have completed all the questions. Check your spelling.'
* Introduce tasks so pupils have to stop and think about the requirements. For instance ask the pupils to:

- say how many tasks are on the worksheet
- circle the key words in the question
- make a chart and check off when parts of the task are complete
- estimate the time needed to complete each task and the whole assignment.

✱ Use highlighting, bold print, underlining and colour to draw the pupils' attention to important information on worksheets, curriculum materials, assignments and tests.

- Remind pupils to stop and think as an important part of following the rules.
- Use Appendix Form 37: 'Pupil reward cards' to recognise and encourage pupils' efforts to stop and think.

Having pupils practice restraint

✱ Use a stopwatch to show impulsive pupils how they often try to give answers instantly. Encourage them to take a few seconds of thinking time before answering or raising their hands.

✱ Have pupils write down the answer before raising their hands. This can help impulsive pupils refrain from shouting out, while at the same time, allowing them to instantly record their answers.

✱ When asking the pupils questions in class, allow plenty of time for thinking: 'I'll ask you to raise your hands in a moment. Right now, think about it carefully, so you are ready when I ask for answers.'

✱ When asking the pupils questions in class, invite pupils to rethink their initial answers: 'Okay now, I can see plenty of hands up. I'll give you a few seconds more to think about your answers before I choose someone.'

✱ Look at the response times of people being interviewed on TV or radio to convince your pupils that good answers are not always instant.

✱ Play review games, where pupils take turns answering the easy questions orally. Do not allow pupils to call out the answer until you drop your finger to show that three seconds have gone by.

✱ Uses games and activities where pupils have to think and plan to get the best result. Chess, card games, writing rough drafts and so forth can work well.

✱ Provide 'speaker cards' to help pupils take their turn at speaking in class. Each pupil receives an allocation of cards that entitle them to speak during group time. If a pupil wishes to speak, they must hold their card in the air and wait until called upon. When the pupil has used up their allocation of cards, they have also used up their turns to speak and must wait for a new allocation. Some pupils become better at 'budgeting' their use of the cards.

✱ Play a game where pupils call out answers to questions orally, but add a twist. For example, when using simple mental arithmetic questions, whenever the answer is nine, the pupils must say 'rhubarb' instead. If a pupil says 'nine', then they are out of the game. This encourages the pupil to slow down and think.

✱ Have activities where pupils are required to make sudden and complete stops in what they are doing. For example, you could play Statues, where on a signal, everyone has to freeze in position and hold it.

✱ If you catch a pupil just about to do the wrong thing, ask him to 'Stop, think, and make a good choice', rather than just telling them to stop what they are doing.

✱ Make clear statements about how much restraint is needed. Do not say, 'Would you mind waiting just one moment', if what you mean is, 'I need you to wait until I have finished this. It could take 10 minutes or so.' The impulsive pupil will wait a moment and then feel quite justified in interrupting you.

✱ Help pupils to develop restraint by giving positive instructions. Instructions to do something are easier to follow than instructions not to do something. So always try to describe the desired behavior ('Stand still') instead of saying what not to do ('Stop running').

✳ If punishment is needed, make it a natural consequence of the behaviour, and have it follow as quickly as possible after the incident.

✳ Do not expect parents to curb their children's impulsive behaviour at school by giving them punishments at home. Consequences need to follow through quickly and in the context where the mistake occurred.

Pupil finds it hard to concentrate

Concentration and organisation observation chart: section 3

3. Pupil finds it hard to concentrate

Pupil often looks around and fidgets when supposed to be listening

Pupil loses concentration when working on a task

Pupil does not see things through to the finish and frequently does not complete the task

Pupil starts one thing and gets sidetracked with something else

Pupil pays attention to distractions instead of concentrating on task

Pupil is inattentive and seems to be in a dream

Pupil sometimes does not appear to have heard what is said

Pupil does not respond to time pressures

Pupil seems vague and unaware of what is going on in the classroom

Pupil does not follow instructions

Pupil starts something but then drifts off task

Some pupils are active, restless and easily distracted. These pupils may be impulsive, always ready to move their attention to whatever new is happening. In some ways, they may seem over-alert, as they are always ready to notice something new. A hundred and one small details seem to divert them from what they are supposed to be doing. Everything attracts their attention, and nothing is filtered out.

On the other hand, some pupils seem to lack alertness. They may gaze around them, apparently oblivious of what is happening. When asked a question, they may seem startled and unsure of what has gone on before. They seem to tune out completely.

Inattentive pupils can often seem in a world of their own. They move at much the same speed, regardless of whether they are supposed to be hurrying or not. They may take a long time to begin a task and then work slowly at their own pace. All too often, they may not finish the assigned task. There are some special reasons for pupils being inattentive and perhaps in a world of their own.

Some very bright pupils may be deeply involved in their own thoughts – imagining, thinking or creating. These bright pupils may be bored by the general classroom work and find their inner world a much more engaging place to be.

At the other end of the scale, pupils with intellectual or language disabilities may be out of their depth with the classroom activities and thus fail to connect with what is going on.

Depressed and worried children and adolescents can also be preoccupied and deep in their own thoughts. School may be of little importance in comparison to the worries with which they may be dealing.

A range of medical difficulties can also cause a pupil to be inattentive in class. A pupil may have a hearing problem. Most hearing difficulties occur in selected frequencies, so the pupil may be able to hear part of every word but have difficulties making sense of what has been said. In this situation, the pupil often tunes out and stops making any attempt to listen.

Epilepsy is a surprisingly common cause of inattentiveness. Pupils may have very brief, but frequent, lapses of consciousness, which can be hard to detect in the classroom. Many cases of mild epilepsy probably go undetected and are treated as inattentiveness. Doctors can assess any pupils suspected of this condition.

Pupils who are unwell or tired may also be apathetic, vague and slow in class. Obviously, it is important to investigate further if the pupil seems to be unduly inattentive, especially if it is not typical of the pupil's usual behavior.

Strategies for managing concentration difficulties

Checking for medical problems

* Get the pupil's hearing checked if there is any doubt.
* If you think that the pupil may be depressed or anxious, discuss your concerns with the parents. Seek further advice from an appropriately qualified professional, such as a doctor or psychologist.
* Ask parents to have a doctor examine any pupil who seems unusually distractible, inattentive or vague.

Matching the curriculum to the pupil

* An inattentive pupil might be very bright and bored. If this seems likely, provide more interesting and challenging work, and monitor the pupil's response.
* If the pupil seems to be struggling with classwork, consider having the pupil assessed to clarify what type of curriculum would be more appropriate.

Providing support and monitoring

* Provide support and close monitoring to help the pupil stay with the task. Give quiet reminders when the pupil is inattentive.
* Have the pupil sit close to the teacher, with a clear view of the teacher's face.
* Use Appendix Form 37: 'Pupil reward cards' to encourage on-task behaviour.
* Use a range of rewards as incentive for task completion.
* Look for examples of strong concentration. Praise the pupil when this occurs.
* Try to ignore irritating but essentially harmless inattentiveness.
* Have pupils monitor their own concentration with the use of note cards. Set a timer, and when it rings, pupils should ask themselves 'Was I concentrating when the timer sounded?' If they were on task, they write *Yes* on the card. If they were not on task, the card is marked *No*.
* Keep a collection of reminder cards in your pocket. This reminder card can be used for any goal the pupil is working towards. This silent reminder card is placed on the pupil's desk to break into periods where the pupil seems to be 'miles away'.
* Often standing quietly beside a pupil can be a sufficient reminder that concentration is required.
* Have 'secret codes' to let pupils know when they need to pay attention or when you think they are doing well. Use a prearranged signal, such as putting a pencil on the pupil's desk, to signify that the pupil needs to attend to the task at hand.
* Create videos of important lessons, and keep them as references. You can build up a library with colleagues as a resource for pupils who need to repeat a lesson for any reason.
* Some pupils listen better if they can doodle or manipulate a small ball or eraser when required to listen. Try this to see if it helps your inattentive pupils listen better.
* Some pupils find it hard to tune in when the teacher transitions between speaking to individuals and speaking to the entire class. Have a signal, such as a bell, to let pupils know when they should stop what they are doing and listen to what you have to say.
* Allow extra time for pupils who are slow or easily distracted to finish a piece of work to a satisfactory standard.
* Give pupils help in summarising what has been taught, in case they have missed something.

Reducing distractions

* Have pupils keep their desktops clear, except for the books and materials needed for a task.
* Create personal workstations. A three-sided screen placed on the desk can cut out distractions and help pupils focus.
* Seat the pupil away from visual distractions such as a corridor window.
* Seat the pupil away from auditory distractions such as the air conditioner, aquarium pump and the like.
* Offer pupils the option of a single desk. Many pupils prefer this.
* Provide blocks of time where pupils work or read quietly without any interaction with each other or the teacher.
* Establish a quiet, working atmosphere in your classroom.
* Avoid distracting visual displays such as mobiles. Have a special place to display creative work that does not intrude into work spaces.
* Play calming music while pupils settle down.
* Consider using a radio loop. The pupil wears the earpiece and the teacher has a microphone, so the teacher's voice is delivered directly to the pupil, cutting out background noise.
* Use noise-cancelling headsets to cut out distracting background noise.

Structuring tasks

* Break large tasks into smaller sections that are more easily completed in a short timeframe.
* Draw a diagram of your lesson plan and mark off steps as you proceed, so pupils find it easier to connect with what you are doing.
* Use graphics to show the 'road map' or diagram of how a task is structured, so pupils can see how much they have completed and what is still ahead.
* Back up verbal instructions with bulleted points on the board, so that once you have finished speaking, pupils can refer back to the written points, if needed.
* Provide an overview of the lesson before you start, and summarise it at the end. Clarify expected learning outcomes, and check that they have been achieved.
* Provide a list of questions that you are going to ask at the end of the session. Write the questions on the board for pupils to refer to. This helps pupils to listen carefully, as they have specific information that they need to know.
* Use theme tunes to signal changes in activity. For instance, have a special tune that is played for the first few minutes of each task, while pupils get organised and settle down to work. By the time the tune is faded out, all pupils should be in their seats and working. Another tune signals the last five minutes of the task, when pupils should be preparing for the next activity.
* Have a definite start time when pupils are asked to start writing. Give a minute or two of thinking time and then a clear signal that writing time has begun.
* Provide prompts and reminders to keep on task: 'Ten minutes left. I will give you another reminder when there are only five minutes left to finish.'

Providing information and training to improve concentration

* Brainstorm with the class to determine methods of concentration. Often you will find pupils use self-talk to remind themselves of priorities.
* Teach the pupils to use self-talk to stay on task: 'I will keep going until I finish. ... If I can concentrate on this for five minutes, I will be finished. ... I lost concentration there for a minute. Better get back on track.'

✳ Have pupils create motivating notices to be displayed at their workstations. Slogans such as *Just do it!* or *Work hard! Work smart!* can help pupils to keep on track.

✳ Help pupils to practise ignoring distractions. Provide a simple task that requires concentration, and try as many fun ways as you can think of to distract them from the task. Challenge their idea that they 'cannot' concentrate!

✳ Be sure you have eye contact with pupils, and that pupils can observe your face as you talk.

✳ Talk to the pupils about what good listening usually looks like (i.e., looking at the speaker, having an alert expression, responding quickly to questions). Have the pupils 'act as if' they are listening to experience a contrast between this and what might be their usual style of inattentive behaviour.

✳ Introduce activities where alertness and quick reactions are essential. For example, have the pupils throw a bean bag to each other, calling the name of the next person to make the catch. Make it more challenging by having two or three bags being thrown around, so the action is fast and pupils have to stay alert.

✳ Provide practice in working quickly with activities that are judged by speed and volume: 'How many words can you write in two minutes?'

✳ Give the pupils frequent physical activity. This can get the circulation going and help pupils to re-energise. It also helps to work off pent-up energy.

✳ Set a timer or stop watch to help pupils work faster for shorter periods of time.

✳ Use dictation as an activity to help pupils develop skills in sustained listening and writing without pauses.

Making it worthwhile for pupils to listen

✳ Vary your teaching style and your voice. Colorful and engaging styles help pupils maintain their interest. Be unpredictable, and have fun with what you do.

✳ Do not endlessly repeat yourself. If you do, pupils will ignore what you say, because they know you will say it again (and again and again!). Make sure pupils know that they need to listen right now! 'Listen carefully, as I am only going to say this once.'

✳ Have a pupil repeat what you have just said to give extra emphasis.

✳ To add variety, ask pupils, instead of the teacher, to read the class announcements.

✳ Allow plenty of pupil action in your class to stimulate involvement.

Allowing for some quiet reflection

✳ Some pupils do need periods of quiet reflection and 'dreaming', so sometimes allow for this in the programme for these pupils.

✳ Some pupils work to maintain alertness and focus in the classroom but need quiet, unhurried time at recess. Create a quiet spot as a haven for those pupils.

Pupil is poorly organised

Concentration and organisation observation chart: section 4

4. Pupil is poorly organised

Pupil is often unprepared, because pupil has not planned ahead

Pupil leaves things until the last minute

Pupil loses things such as school work, materials or clothing

Pupil forgets to bring materials and books when they are needed

Pupil is messy; does not keep papers, materials and supplies in order

Pupil misses deadlines for handing in work

Some pupils seem to be in a permanent muddle. Important materials are lost, papers are mislaid and assignments are late. The pupils' desks, backpacks and lockers are always a mess. These pupils often fail to demonstrate their potential because of poor organisation. They may have very good intentions to stay on top of the work, but because of poor planning and time management, they end up in chaos.

These pupils often have 'time blindness.' They have a poor sense of time. They misjudge how long a task will take. They do not realise how few days remain before a task must be finished. Often they leave things until the very last minute, hopeful that they will have plenty of time. Sometimes work is finished, but it is lost or forgotten and not handed in on time.

Pupils also may think that other people's good organisation just 'happens' and that their own lack of organisation is due to unexpected circumstances. They may also be overly optimistic, always sure that the library will have the book they need right away, that the equipment they need will be waiting for them on the shelf, that the printer will keep working and that they will be able to complete the assignment in record time.

Poorly organised pupils will often spend too much time on trivial elements of a task, such as decorating the title page, and do not leave enough time for the rest.

Strategies for working with organisation

Monitoring and supporting

* Have an adult support the pupil to ensure that organisation is monitored and assisted if needed.
* Create groups where pupils support one another with daily organisation.
* Give all pupils equal opportunity to take responsibility in the class and in the school. If necessary, support the pupil in the organisation of the duties required.
* Assign an 'organisation partner' to help with organisation.
* Set aside time each day for the pupils to organise themselves and their possessions. Keeping desks, school bags and lockers neat and tidy is a good start.
* Set aside time weekly to more fully organise desks, bags and lockers. Pupils can use this time to discard unnecessary items and organise the remaining materials.
* Insert two minutes of thinking time at the end of the school day. Pupils must sit still and use the time to think: 'What do I need to take home with me? What do I have to remember to do when I get home? What day is it today? Is there anything special I need to remember for tomorrow?'
* Suggest that parents impose a similar thinking time before the pupils leave home: 'Have I got all my stuff? Did I check my assignment book?'
* Check the pupil's study assignment at the end of the school day to make sure all the important information is written down.
* Where possible, ask rather than tell pupils: 'What do you need to remember for tomorrow? How are you going to make sure you don't forget? Tell me what material you will need to bring with you.'
* Quickly identify pupils who are behind schedule or who are late in completing their work. Help these pupils to catch up before they fall too far behind.

Organising the classroom

* Have a clear routine in your classroom, so there is predictability.
* Be very explicit about what is required of the pupils. Make definite statements, and stick to the rules you make so that pupils know where they stand.
* Be organised yourself, so that you set a good example.

✳ Provide pupils with an organised learning programme. Think ahead, and plan appropriate modifications from the start. Try not to change instructions or expectations once pupils have started on a task.

✳ Manage class time so that pupils are not rushed. Allow time for planning, checking, general organisation and administration.

✳ Invest time in making your classroom neat and well organised, so pupils can find and store things quickly and easily. Clean up often and avoid letting things become out of order or cluttered.

✳ Have a definite place (a labeled box or tray) where pupils place finished work.

✳ Have a planner on the classroom wall, and refer to it often as you indicate what is expected of the pupils in terms of organisation: 'See, here we are today, and your assignment is due in on Friday, the day after tomorrow. So you have just one day left to get it finished.'

Developing good organisation

✳ Brainstorm in the class to share ideas about how to get organised.

✳ Make a poster of things that 'smart thinkers' do to organise themselves, and have it clearly displayed in the classroom. Use visual illustrations to give quick visual prompts.

✳ Have pupils figure out what has gone wrong in situations where they were poorly organised. Did they misjudge the time needed? Did they lose something? Did they forget?

✳ Listen to the pupils' excuses about what went wrong with their organisation, and then use Appendix Form 34: 'Pupil plan for getting organised' to help pupils plan better strategies next time.

✳ Have the pupils write a reminder list of good strategies to keep on display. Get the pupil to make the list highly visible with graphics, colour and decoration. Find a very prominent place to put the list.

✳ Have fun with the ideas. Get the class to suggest zany reasons for good organisation. Here are some to get you started:
  • papers that are not put in a folder will get stolen by aliens
  • work left until the last minute turns into the Hulk
  • lockers can turn into black holes in the universe unless you keep them tidy.

✳ Make organisation part of the task requirements: 'Make a folder with four sections. List the materials needed. Write a checklist of all the things you need to do for this task.' Consider grading pupils for meeting these basic requirements. This will help pupils see that organisation is an important part of what they have to do.

✳ Have pupils use a task planner on a computer, which provides task-specific reminders several days before something is due.

✳ Encourage pupils to identify priorities and focus on them. Encourage pupils to make a list of what needs to be done, and number the items in order of importance. The pupil then starts with the top priority task first. You can use Appendix Form 32: 'Pupil priorities chart' to help with this.

✳ Have pupils challenge themselves to complete an assignment the day before it is actually due, so they have a spare day if needed.

✳ Help pupils to schedule work so they are able to meet the deadlines. As well as entering the due date, have them select the day they will start, dates when they plan to have completed the various sections of the work and the date they plan to have their final draft ready for revision and editing. You can use the Appendix Form 31: 'Pupil work planner' to help with this.

✳ Ask pupils to show you their personal timetables for tackling a big task, such as a final test review or a large project. Ask pupils to check in with you daily to keep you up-to-date on their progress.

* Create a group or class timetable for large projects, where all pupils check off their individual progress. Pupils lagging behind can see what is happening.
* Get your pupils to 'expect the unexpected', and build this into their timetable/plan so that they have a margin when the inevitable setback occurs.
* Link a routine task (such as putting up your chair at the end of the day) with an organisational task (such as running through a checklist of what to take home). Help pupils to build organisation into their daily routines.

Managing paperwork and equipment

* Keep a list of homework assignments on the class website. Pupils can log on, view the list and download it if necessary.
* Encourage pupils to submit assignments electronically to avoid work being finished and then lost.
* Have pupils keep one large file that holds every piece of loose paper they are currently working on. Help the pupil set up the file with appropriate sections.
* Have pupils make themselves a 'Home–School' plastic zip file. It is brightly coloured, decorated and easy to find. All notices to take home, all notes from parents to the teacher and other important documents and reminders go into this file. The file is checked by the pupil (with adult prompting, if needed) at the start of each school day and when the pupil gets home at night.
* Worksheets that are not hole-punched hardly ever get filed. Hole-punch worksheets before they are given out, or have pupils carry a small hole punch with them.
* Have a spare set of basic materials (pencil, ruler, calculator, etc.) that pupils can use when they cannot find their own.
* If pupils become too dependent on borrowing from you, ask the pupils to give you something of their own each time they borrow. When the teacher's item is returned, the pupil receives his own possession back.
* Colour code books to help identification.
* If the pupil has an exercise book for each subject, then either hole-punch each book and place them all in a large file, or use a concertina file to keep all the exercise books together.
* Teach good filing skills, so pupils do not lose information that is stored outside of their minds! Provide suitable filing systems, such as alphabetical folders, accordion files, filing cabinets and the like.
* Teach good organisation of computer files, using proper folders and accurate file naming when saving.
* Make sure pupils have their computers set to save work automatically and at frequent intervals.
* Have pupils get in the habit of backing up everything they do on the computer.

Concluding Chapter 5

This chapter has discussed the fact that some pupils have great difficulties with concentration and organization, even if their motivation and intentions are good. They can't seem to help themselves. The strategies presented here will help not only those pupils who have real problems in these areas, but also those who could just use a little boost. Everyone has times when it's difficult to concentrate, and all pupils can benefit from developing habits of organisation that will help them throughout lives.

Chapter 6

Teamwork

Introduction

Teaching is a team effort. In this chapter, we look at how we can work together with professional colleagues to create a school community where inclusion is welcomed as the *fair and reasonable thing to do.*

Inclusion of pupils without the inclusion of their parents just does not make sense, so we also must explore the importance of understanding parents' perspectives, respecting their needs and including them as important members of the team.

The following forms from the Appendix are referred to in this chapter:

Appendix Form 25: 'Teacher: personal profile as an inclusive teacher'
Appendix Form 28: 'Teacher notes: getting ready for a meeting'
Appendix Form 39: 'Pupil's notes: getting ready for a meeting'
Appendix Form 42: 'Parent notes: getting ready for a meeting'
Appendix Form 29: 'Teacher: meeting record'.

Teamwork with professional colleagues

Creating an inclusive school community

Inclusion is the law, but that's just the beginning of the story. A real commitment to meet the needs of all pupils through an inclusive school programme goes beyond the letter of the law. Often it is the small, intuitive, personal choices made by adults and pupils within a school community that reflect true inclusiveness. Often it is not so much what you do as how you do it!

> 'As soon as we arrived, I could tell it was going to be fine. They did not treat us like we were asking for anything extra, only that they wanted to know all about Zoe, so they could help her fit in with the other kids. The other school made it seem like we were asking too much. They made it sound like they were doing us a big favour.'

School leadership, policy development and ongoing professional training are all important elements in the development and maintenance of an inclusive school community. Individual commitment from every teacher and strong teamwork are the other essential ingredients in an inclusive school.

Effective intervention also needs a coordinated and positive group effort, from planning to implementation and evaluation. Meeting individual needs is an ongoing process that will involve many members of the school community working together.

Parents and pupils will see the end result of good teamwork and communication skills. Of course, they will also notice when teamwork or communication are ineffective!

Here are some things that parents noticed and worried about:

- 'Last year the teacher and I worked it all out. She made quite a few changes to how she taught him, and it worked very well. This year, the teacher did not know anything about what happened last year. I don't think she had even looked in his file or spoken to the teacher from the previous year.'
- 'When we have a meeting with the specialists and the teacher and the headmaster everything sounds fine. But really once it gets down to what actually happens in the classroom, it's nothing like we agreed at the meeting.'
- 'We go to lots of meetings and I can tell that the teachers don't see eye-to-eye with each other. There's one teacher, Mr Gladstone, who is really keen to help. But whatever he suggests the other teacher says it can't be done, or it's too hard, or it is "not appropriate", whatever that means.'
- 'He has two teachers, Mandy on Monday and Tuesday and Ted for the rest of the week. The trouble is they have such different ways of doing things, so what is OK on Monday is all wrong on Wednesday. My son can't cope with that. He has enough trouble dealing with one set of rules.'
- 'The classroom teacher does a very good job, but when she was away, he was always in trouble. Then I found out that the substitute teacher had not been given any information about him or his difficulties.'
- 'My son does have an unusual disability, but last year was fantastic. Faye, his teacher, had received special training in just that area. But this year it's really frustrating. His new teacher was really offended when I asked if Faye could come to the meeting. This teacher says she can handle it herself. I think she's afraid to admit that she does not have the same expertise as Faye.'

Strategies for working with teaching colleagues

Creating an inclusive school community

- ✳ Openly endorse the right of every pupils, parent and colleague to equal and appropriate treatment, not only because it is the law but because it is the *fair and reasonable thing to do.*
- ✳ Check your own profile as an inclusive teacher. Use Appendix Form 25: 'Teacher: personal profile as an inclusive teacher'. Seek out professional development opportunities, such as courses, books and conferences to further your knowledge.
- ✳ Always treat inclusion and intervention as integral and essential parts of everything you do. Avoid implying or even thinking that intervention strategies are 'extras' you have to do on top of your 'real' work.
- ✳ Emphasise that the school community is a single social unit. Every pupil, every parent and every staff member is included in the group. Celebrate anniversaries, achievements and special occasions together.
- ✳ Have informal social gatherings to share fun and friendship with everyone connected with your school.
- ✳ Use *our* instead of *the* to stress the fact that everyone belongs and shares in the school community. *Our school, our library, our helpers.*
- ✳ Make a celebration of diversity. Highlight the fact that *everyone* is unique and that a mix of abilities, talents, difficulties and differences is normal.
- ✳ Create a collage of photographs that includes every pupil and adult in the school. As soon as someone new arrives, include that person's photograph in the group picture.
- ✳ Do not tolerate 'put downs' of any pupil, parent or colleague, even in the privacy of the teachers' room or 'teachers only' meetings. Such statements immediately create

a division between 'us' and 'them'. Comments made should always be professional, inclusive, respectful and nonjudgemental.

- Use 'I statements' when talking about colleagues, parents or pupils, such as: 'I found it difficult to explain how the programme will work.'
- 'I don't think I have earned his trust yet.'

✳ Avoid using words such as *pushy, angry, anxious, difficult* and *negative,* which place blame on a colleague or parent. Try to rephrase words to show the other side of the story:

- Pushy could mean she does not trust us to do the right thing
- Angry could mean he is feeling powerless and frustrated
- Anxious could mean she is afraid and needs a lot of reassurance
- Difficult could mean we have not looked at it from his perspective
- Negative could mean she has a sense of hopelessness about this.

✳ Do not allow prejudice, gossip, bias or exclusion to go unchallenged or unchecked.

Leadership

✳ Create a 'can do' culture, where finding positive ways of meeting challenges is the norm.

✳ Recognise and celebrate achievements in good teaching, where intervention and inclusive practices are part of the success story.

✳ Encourage team members to ask for help, share expertise and work together to maximise inclusive practices and interventions.

✳ Set up interest groups, advisory groups, mentor systems and goal-directed teams to contribute to inclusion and intervention.

✳ Model inclusive behaviours in your relationships with pupils, colleagues and parents.

✳ Actively encourage ongoing professional development so that team members can continually improve their skills related to intervention and inclusive practices.

✳ Follow through with team decisions, and support those required to implement them in the classroom.

✳ Deal with interpersonal differences that impact the teachers' abilities to provide interventions for the pupils.

✳ Make sure administrative systems are in place, so information about pupils and their needs can be effectively communicated to all teachers.

Teamwork

✳ Teaching is a demanding job that can be stressful. Support your colleagues with care, concern and practical assistance when the going gets tough.

✳ Ask for support and assistance from your colleagues, supervisors and administrators, if you are finding that your work is too stressful.

✳ Take care of yourself! If you are exhausted, unwell, depressed, anxious or overly stressed, you will not be able to provide the pupils or your colleagues with the support they need.

✳ Follow through with what has been agreed upon by the group. Do not say one thing in a group meeting and then do something different once the meeting is over.

✳ You do not have to be an instant expert on everything. Talk to colleagues, and share expertise both ways. If you do not know something, say so and then find someone who can help or provide the information that you need.

✳ Make time for regular meetings with colleagues. You cannot work together unless you spend time talking together.

✳ Be flexible and accommodating and a good team player.

✳ Be prepared to pull your weight. Be generous with your time, effort and expertise to make inclusive education and intervention a success story in your school.

✳ Communicate with your colleagues and coordinate what you do, so pupils and parents have continuity between one teacher and another.
✳ Be particularly careful during transition periods, such as changes from one school year to the next, so that all information is shared with the next teacher.
✳ Have regular 'show and tell' sessions, where colleagues report back from conferences, present professional papers, describe examples of good practice and generally enhance the team's ability to be inclusive and provide effective intervention.
✳ Share resources that individual teachers develop in class. You could include:
  • teacher-made materials, such as worksheets that can be copied and used again
  • audiotape and reading book packages
  • resource folders that support pupils with projects on specific topics
  • classroom posters
  • classroom pets and plants.

Working with parents

When a pupil experiences difficulties in school, parent reactions may vary. Some parents will immediately do everything they can to support the teachers, other parents may blame the school, and yet others may appear very anxious, defensive or demanding.

Learning difficulties often create friction and upset at home. The parent may need to deal with a child who is anxious, depressed, angry or distressed because of difficulties in school. Some pupils may show physical signs of emotional disturbance, such as bedwetting, poor sleeping or poor eating. Others may become emotionally volatile or withdrawn in response to their day-to-day difficulties in school.

Parents may become genuinely concerned that their child faces a future with seriously limited prospects for employment, independence and a fulfilling life. Family patterns can give a dramatically different slant on the situation.

Some parents may fear that failure at school may push their child towards substance abuse, suicide or anti-social behavior. Sometimes, the level of the pupil's distress is not seen or even suspected by teachers at school.

  • 'My brother was exactly the same [as my son] when he was at school. He ended up on the wrong side … juvenile detention and then jail … never has had a proper job … in and out of jail all his life. I just hope and pray that Joel won't go the same way.'
  • 'Sometimes I feel real guilty. … It was in my family and now I've passed it on to my kids.'
  • 'He's Mr Cool in school. He would hate for the other kids to see him upset. But at home he is cranky, says he is "hopeless" and that he "would be better off dead". He really scares me sometimes.'
  • 'They say I worry too much. But I don't know what else to do. If I don't worry about her, who will?'

A pupil's difficulties at school can also create friction within the family. Parents can blame each other, and siblings can resent the extra attention given to the brother or sister with learning difficulties.

'Eric just won't accept that his son isn't at the top of the class, so there's no let up. "Make him do extra work … make him try harder … tell him to do it again." Eric just won't listen to me and give the kid a break. The other kids get fed up too. "When are you going to help me? It's not fair he gets all the help." To be honest, it's all getting too much for me to cope with.'

Parents as part of the team

The law states that parents must be informed and involved in all aspects of their children's education. Indeed, how could one imagine that the pupils is included if the parent is *ex*cluded?

Parents are the real experts with their own child. Not only do they know the pupil better than anyone else, they also care more than anyone else. Their influence on the pupil is likely to be much stronger than the teachers' and their involvement will be lifelong. On the other hand, teachers have professional expertise and experience. It is obvious that a partnership between these two expert groups is going to be part of the future.

But how does this partnership between school and parents work in practice?

Parents sometimes find that dealing with school is a challenge. Maybe their personal school experiences were negative. Perhaps they lack the skills or confidence needed to deal with teachers, systems and situations. Some parents may not understand their child's rights and may feel ashamed of the demands that are placed on teachers; others may have unrealistic expectations of what teachers and school systems can provide.

Even if parents lack skills or understanding, doing nothing may not be an option for them. Parents often have a strong drive to help their child and will often find a way to do the best they can. They may search the Internet and come up with unreliable information. They may be sucked into inappropriate therapies or try to invent their own do-it-yourself programme at home.

Likewise, teachers find that working in partnership with parents demands skill, tact, time and patience. Teachers need to be flexible to work with a wide range of parents, all with different expectations, skills and circumstances. It is all too easy to misjudge parents on the basis of preconceived ideas, prejudices or limited understanding. The following expressions of parental concern provide a little insight into how some parents react to their children's difficulties and the teacher's role.

- 'I still feel like I am a kid waiting to be told off by the teacher.'
- 'I ask the teachers how I can help, but they say he is doing well and that they can handle it. But I want to be sure I have done all I can, so I've just bought this very expensive computer program. It was a lot more than we could afford, but the salesman said it will definitely make him an A class pupil.'
- 'They say she has developmental delay, so I can't understand why she is still doing little kids' stuff if she needs to catch up.'
- 'When they tell me all the trouble he is having, I feel really bad, like he is making a lot of extra work for the teachers … and they are busy people. I've told him … don't keep bothering the teacher.'
- 'The teachers tell me all this stuff about her, like it's my fault. I tell them I'm not educated myself and I can't be there to see what she is doing in class. It's hard enough when she comes home from school and she's got all that work to do … it's way beyond me. My reading isn't so good and they teach things differently now.'
- 'The teachers never told me about the special programme running over the holidays. I guess they knew I wouldn't be able to afford it. But my boss knew about the programme because his son has been on it the year before. He said the company had a special fund to help employees' families, and so both the kids went. … It was great for them.'

Communication between home and school

Inclusive education and intervention only work effectively when *everyone* is well informed.

Teachers need to understand the big picture before they have enough information to plan an effective programme in school. What can the parents tell the teacher about the pupil?

Are there family circumstances that make a difference? What are the parents' priorities? What are the pupil's main concerns? Why isn't inclusive education working as well as you had hoped? How can the intervention programme be improved?

Parents, too, need to have information. 'How are the teachers helping my child? How does that work? What can I do to help? How is my child doing? What will happen next year? '

The exchange of information between home and school may be inadequate for a variety of reasons, such as poor communication skills, lack of time, discontinuity of teachers or poorly established communication channels.

Parents may feel frustrated and anxious, because they do not understand what teachers are doing to help their child. A good inclusive education programme is often seamless. Students and adults work together, and special intervention and strategies are an integral part of the classroom. The downside of this is that parents may not 'see' the programme at all, as there are no visits to the special education room and no separate work folders or time spent working alone on 'special' work.

- 'Those teachers are all so educated … half the time I don't make any sense of what they are saying to me. "Oh don't you worry, Mrs Goldsmith", they say. "We've got the SENCO" and I don't know what else besides, I really don't understand half of it.'
- 'I kept asking him, "Did you get any extra help today?" and he kept saying, "No, I just stayed in the classroom like I always do." So I went up to the school, ready to have a real fight. But then the teacher shows me her class record. Every day the teacher's helper has been working with him in the class. It is all written down, there's a file of work he's already done and there's plenty more to come. So they have been doing a really good job, but they hadn't told me the detail, and Tom didn't see it as anything special. I had to apologise to the teacher for thinking she wasn't doing her job.'
- 'Every year the teachers say, "It will click. Don't worry. He is making progress." But I can see that he is so far behind the other children that he will never catch up.'
- 'The teacher says to write a note, but my writing and spelling is shameful … so I don't do that. I just tell her to tell the teacher … but I reckon she forgets.'

Strategies for working with parents

The parents' perspective

* Recognise that a family's cultural and religious values and traditions may play a significant part in the parents' perspective.
* Remember that parents often see a different side of their child compared to the one you see at school. Always talk to them about how things are at home and their personal concerns about the pupil.
* Anxiety is a normal and healthy reaction to a problem. It stimulates action and problem solving. Work with anxious parents to deal with the problems they perceive.
* Do not dismiss parents' anxieties as unfounded because you think the problem is minor. Respect parental concerns, and do all you can to address them.
* Parents will be particularly anxious if they do not know or understand the full picture. Provide as much information as you can and help to interpret it, so that parents have an accurate picture of the situation and what is being done to work with the problem.
* Parents, too, have a lot of information about their child. Ask parents to discuss their child and to help you to see things through the eyes of the pupils and the family.
* Sometimes, parents have had unfortunate experiences in previous encounters with professionals. You do not have to judge or defend your colleagues, but you do need to understand the issues that the parents are dealing with. So say to them: 'Things do

not always go well. Looking back, what have been the worst situations for you or for your child?'

* Other times, parents have had very positive experiences with professionals. Knowing what has worked well in the past and what the parents find most helpful is an important part of future planning. So ask parents: 'What has worked really well in the past? ... When did you feel things were going well?'
* Remember that there may be a family history that colours the parents' reactions to difficulties with learning.
* Do not take parental concern or questioning about a pupil's progress as a personal attack on your professional skills as a teacher. Parents have a right to ask questions, express concern and obtain as much information as they can about their child.
* Let parents know that you hear and understand their perspective. Rephrase what they have told you, and reflect it back to them: 'So your main concern is with her reading.' Sometimes they will need to correct you, if you have misunderstood.
* Do not make the parents feel that they are to blame for the pupil's difficulties.
* Make sure that parents have the support they need to understand and support their child. Provide extra counselling, discussion and practical help to ease tensions, if they exist.
* Talk to parents about the pressures that the pupil's learning difficulties place on the family. Do what you can to relieve the pressure. For example, make sure homework does not require excessive parental involvement, and provide parents with information about community support groups.
* Talk to parents about their thoughts concerning their child's future, so that you understand their hopes and fears.
* Work with the parents to find out about positive avenues that may be available to the pupil in future years. These may be quite different from what you had assumed.
* Share with parents the positives as well as the negatives about the pupil.

Parents as part of the team

* Do whatever you can to make parents feel that *your* school is *their* school, too. Consult and involve parents in the day-to-day life of the school.
* Invite the parents to bring a support person (relative, neighbour, social worker, friend) when they attend meetings at school.
* Ask parents to select a person on the school staff with whom they feel comfortable. Ask that person to attend school meetings for support and as the parents' advocate.
* Make sure that the parent knows the name and function of each person on the professional team. Provide a written list of names and contact details for the parent.
* When a large number of professionals meet together with parents, make sure that the professionals include the parents in the discussion and do not leave them on the sidelines.
* Have one member of the meeting monitor the discussion and 'translate' any professional exchanges that the parents may not understand: 'IEP stands for Individualised Education Programme, so that means it is an individual programme that we will work out especially for Sarah Jane.'
* Help parents to work with you rather than seek outside help (such as possibly dubious 'educational' products or perhaps poorly qualified 'therapists'). Provide the parents with the guidance and resources to enable them to work successfully with their child.
* Some parents are unable to contribute to the team in any practical way. This does not mean that they do not want to know what is going on and have a say in how things proceed, so include them in the information loop, even if they do not actively participate.

* Parents are not necessarily educational experts. Parents often need help to understand the ongoing nature of their child's difficulties, the reasons the pupil's programme is modified and the purpose of the activities provided.
* Conversely, some parents are very well informed. Accept the information that they bring to you with interest and respect. They may have done some excellent research and have a lot to contribute.
* Even if you think parents are misinformed, you still need to understand what it is they believe to be true, so you can work with them to clarify the issues.
* Invite parents to join the teaching staff at professional conferences where members of the public are able to attend.
* As a teacher, accompany parents to public meetings that relate to the pupil's needs.
* Share professional information with parents. Copy a journal article that might be of interest, lend a book or record a relevant TV programme.
* Create as many opportunities as you can for parents to be involved in the pupil's programme. Invite parents into the classroom, offer them training sessions in how to help and talk to parents often about their child.
* Do not hold back information (for example, about a special programme) because you judge that these parents will not be interested, cannot afford the option, will not be prepared to travel or cannot put in the extra time or similar reasons. Always provide the information, and let the parents decide whether it is suitable for them.

Communication between home and school

Listening

* Communication is a two-way street. *You need to be a good listener* so that parents can communicate with you. Good listening involves a range of skills.

Language

* For parents to be included, everyone must speak the same language. Avoid using jargon or 'buzz' words that will immediately put parents at a disadvantage. Use plain language that everyone can understand.
* Identify the parents' preferred language for communication and use that, if possible. If not, have an interpreter available.

Contact

* Find out the best way to contact the parents. Would they rather you telephoned them at home or at work? What time is best? Do they prefer email or a written note?
* Identify the parent's preferred place for a meeting. Many parents do not like you to visit them at home. Other parents will be pleased for you to call.
* Let parents know how to contact you and your colleagues. Should they telephone the school office with a request that you call them back? Should they email you? Should they write a note? Make sure that the parents have the full range of contact details that will work for them.
* When needed, set up a regular two-way system of communication for regular exchange of information, such as a 'Home–School' book that travels between home and school each day with the pupil, for daily updates from the parent and the teacher.

Table 6.1 Effective communication

Communication skill	Examples of good communication	Examples of poor communication
Positive nonverbal language.	Examples of positive nonverbal language.	Examples of negative nonverbal language.
Appropriate eye contact.	You look at the person you are speaking to. You make eye contact (unless this is culturally inappropriate or seems to make the parent uncomfortable).	You look around the room while they talk. You glance at your watch or computer screen. You look at papers on your desk
Warm and responsive facial expression.	You smile appropriately, you look interested and your face reacts to what is said.	You look bored. You yawn. Your face does not register the appropriate emotion.
Body posture reflects interest and involvement.	You lean slightly forward. You look relaxed and open.	You look defensive: your arms are folded tightly across your chest. You look aggressive: you point your finger at them to make a point. You look uninterested: you fiddle with papers or pens.
Respectful and caring attitude	Examples of respectful and caring attitude.	Examples of disrespectful and uncaring attitude
You are aware of cultural, religious or racial differences.	You offer refreshments that meet religious dietary requirements. The decor of your office and your clothing is restrained, tasteful and appropriate.	You offer inappropriate refreshments .You have a potentially offensive poster or slogan on display. Your style of dress could offend.
You know something about the family circumstances.	You remember what the parents told you previously about their family. You have taken time to get some background information.	You clearly know nothing about the family. You have forgotten what they told you last time. You have not even looked at the child's file.
You use the person's preferred name.	The parent has said his name is 'Robert,' and you call him that.	You call the parent 'Bob'. You forget his name or call him the wrong name.
You value the parents' time.	You are on time when you arrange to meet with parents.	You are late. You forget the appointment.
Empathetic listening.	Examples of good empathetic listening.	Examples of non-empathetic listening
You make time and provide opportunity for the parent to talk.	You ask the parent to come into a quiet room to talk. You arrange to meet later when you can listen properly.	You expect the parent to talk to you while you are supervising pupils. You hold a discussion in a busy corridor where other parents are waiting.
Your phone is on silent.	You pay full attention to the parent and their concerns.	Your phone rings and you take the call.
You have arranged not to be disturbed.	You pay full attention to the parents and their concerns.	You talk to people who come into your room during the meeting.
You reflect the speaker's feelings.	'I can see you are feeling very worried about the new schedule.'	'I think the new schedule will be excellent – no problem at all.'

continued

Table 6.1 continued

Communication skill	Examples of good communication	Examples of poor communication
You express interest by maintaining brief verbal remarks.	'That's tough … I see … did he really … amazing … oh dear … mmm …'	You interrupt and/or talk over the parent.
You rephrase what has been said.	'So you are pretty sure that the other kids were mostly to blame.'	You shift to a new topic as if you have not heard what the parent said.
You summarise what has been said.	'Basically, there are two main issues. We need to look at her reading programme and sort out the problems with the mathematics time table.'	You do not clarify what has been discussed. 'Well it was good to meet you. Thank you for coming.'
You accept the parent's situation without judgement.	'I know that often you both have to work late. A lot parents find that is difficult. It's not so easy being a parent sometimes.'	'Of course, if you can't be bothered to get home in time. … Most parents in this school can.'
You give the parents time and space to speak.	You do not always rush in to speak when the parent pauses. You can sit quietly and wait. People will often tell you a lot more if you do this.	You cut the parent off as they speak. As soon as there is a gap in what the parent says, you start to talk. You dominate the meeting and talk most of the time.
Good questioning.	Examples of good questioning	Examples of poor questioning
You ask questions that relate to what the parent has just said.	The parent has just said that they are pleased with the pupils's progress. You ask, 'So what do you think was the reason it worked so well?'	The parent has just said that they are pleased with the pupils's progress. You ask, 'Did I give you that form for the school outing?'
You ask questions that reflect an awareness of the parent's viewpoint.	'I know you prefer Kylie to sit next to Kim, but we would like her next to Jo. Would that be okay?'	'We are going to try to sit Kylie next to Jo. Is that okay?'
You ask open questions that allow the parent scope to answer.	'How do you think things have gone since John started the programme?'	'John has done very well on the programme. Are you pleased?'
You use questions to increase the flow of information.	'Tell me more about. … Can you explain. … What was the background to that … ?'	You close topics too soon before you have all the information. You do not ask enough questions.

Meetings

✳ Parents may never have been to a formal meeting before. Explain what to expect, and offer reassurance and assistance if they seem anxious or uncertain.

✳ Before any meeting, it is a good idea to give everyone the chance to think ahead and plan what they want to say. Appendix Form 28: 'Teacher notes: getting ready for a meeting', Appendix Form 39: 'Pupil notes: getting ready for a meeting' and Appendix Form 42: 'Parent notes: getting ready for a meeting' are forms created for teachers, pupils and parents. You can use these to help everyone be equally prepared.

✳ Prepare an agenda, and circulate it before the meeting. This can range from a simple list of discussion points to a formal agenda.

✳ Ask a person to chair the meeting to make sure that the agenda (however informal) is covered and that everyone has a fair chance to speak.

* If several family members attend a meeting, you may need to help get a balance if one dominates the discussion: 'John, Rachel has told us her concerns. How do you feel about Sam?'
* Allow enough time for a meeting. There is nothing worse for parents than to feel that time is limited and the teacher is in a hurry.
* Finish meetings in an orderly way. Signal when the time is running out, and invite everyone to have their final words.
* If you do run out of time, set a date and time for another meeting to continue the discussion.
* It is important to have a written record of every meeting. Parents often get left out of this process! Invite the parents to make a contribution to the minutes of the meeting or to write and submit their own record. Appendix Form 29: 'Teacher: meeting record' can be used by the teacher, parent or pupils.
* It is useful to compile all the meeting records and to look for discrepancies in people's understanding of the meeting and its outcome. Obviously, any differences need to be dealt with quickly.

Honesty

* Provide parents honest and regular feedback about their child's progress. False reassurance does more harm than good.
* Parents will be particularly anxious if they do not know or understand the full picture. Provide as much information as you have, and help them to interpret it, so they have an accurate picture of the situation and what is being done to work with the problem.
* Keep parents well informed about the intervention and inclusion strategies you are using in the classroom. Because effective and truly inclusive strategies are often virtually 'invisible', parents may not know what is being done unless they are told explicitly.
* Always admit it if you do not know something or you have made a mistake: 'I am really not sure about that. I will find out and let you know. ... Right now things are not going well, so we will need to look at making some changes to his programme. ... I'm afraid I made a mistake, so I will. ...'

Concluding Chapter 6

This chapter has stressed the importance of teachers working with professional colleagues and parents to establish good communication regarding pupils' programmes and their well-being. Everyone has different pieces of the puzzle and all team members, including parents, need to work together and support each other. It's crucial to make no prejudgements or assumptions as to what another member of the team is thinking or feeling. Openness, cooperation and implementing strategies for sharing information will create an atmosphere of trust, make everyone's job easier and support the final goal of helping the pupils thrive.

Appendix

Observation charts

Literacy resources

Mathematics resources

Teaching resources

Pupil support resources

Parent Resources

Form 1 **Reading observation chart**

	Does not apply	Some-times applies	Usually applies	See page
1. Pupil feels negative about reading.				27
Pupil is reluctant to read; will not read without prompting; complains when reading.				
Pupil avoids reading, 'loses' book, tries delaying tactics.				
Pupil becomes angry or upset with reading.				
Pupil tries to avoid reading in front of fellow pupils.				
2. Pupil is disadvantaged by poor reading.				30
Pupil demonstrates difficulty reading materials or textbooks suitable for age group.				
Pupil needs additional time to complete reading tasks compared to peers.				
Pupil does not finish reading assignments in the allotted time.				
Pupil runs out of time in examinations because of slow reading.				
3. Pupil has difficulties with reading.				32
Pupil needs additional time to acquire basic reading skills.				
Pupil achieves less than other pupils in reading.				
Pupil needs more support than others when learning how to read.				
4. Pupil does not understand how reading 'works.'				37
Pupil thinks that reading happens automatically.				
Pupil does not realise that skilled readers have to work hard at times.				
Pupil does not think about own reading strategies.				
5. Pupil has difficulties with phonics.				38
Pupil has difficulties remembering letter shapes.				
Pupil makes errors when sounding out single letters.				
Pupil makes errors when sounding out letter blends.				
6. Pupil has difficulties with phonological awareness and word building.				40
Pupil makes errors when trying to hear sounds in words.				
Pupil makes errors when blending sounds together.				
Pupil makes errors reading new words. (See Appendix Form 6: Diagnostic Phonics Assessment.)				
7. Pupil has difficulties recognising words at sight.				42
Pupil makes errors when attempting to read everyday words.				
Pupil can read words in a familiar book but cannot read the same words out of context.				
Pupil relies on pictures to get sense of story.				

Success with Inclusion © Glynis Hannell, Routledge 2008

Form 1 Reading observation chart *continued*

	Does not apply	Some-times applies	Usually applies	See page
Pupil makes many errors and self-corrections when reading.				
Pupil confuses words of similar appearance, such as bread and bird.				
Pupil makes errors when copying words.				
Pupil reads word by word.				
Pupil puts in different words but keeps the meaning of the story. For example, reads Jane got a present for her birthday instead of Jane got a parcel for her birthday.				
8. Pupil has difficulties with reading fluency.				46
Pupil's oral language is hesitant and lacks fluency.				
Pupil stammers when speaking and reading.				
Pupil cannot find the right word when reading.				
Pupil's reading is hesitant and stilted.				
Pupil takes a long time to recognise words.				
Pupil sounds out the same words over and over again.				
Pupil does not use punctuation to guide reading.				
Pupil reads so slowly that the amount of practice is limited.				
9. Pupil has difficulties making sense of what is read.				48
Pupil puts in words that do not make sense. For example: Jane got a playing for her birthday.				
Pupil makes up words. For example: Jane got a purrel for her birthday.				
Pupil makes errors answering reading comprehension questions.				
10. Pupil may have visual difficulties.				50
Pupil rubs eyes when reading.				
Pupil tilts head when reading.				
Pupil uses finger to keep place when reading.				
Pupil covers one eye with hand when reading.				
Pupil complains of headache when reading.				
Pupil skips words and lines when reading.				
Pupil reads for only a short period of time before needing a break.				
Pupil chooses books with large print.				
11. Pupil has advanced reading skills.				51
Pupil's reading is advanced compared to peer group.				
Pupil complains that reading is boring, even though the pupil reads well.				
Pupil prefers factual books to fiction.				

Form 2 Written language observation chart

	Does not apply	Some-times applies	Usually applies	See page
1. Pupil feels negative about writing.				54
Pupil complains when asked to write.				
Pupil avoids writing whenever possible.				
Pupil's writing is very brief in comparison to peers' work.				
Pupil expresses difficulty in knowing how to start or knowing what to write.				
2. Difficulties with written language impact classroom achievement.				56
Pupil's oral contribution in class is not reflected in written work.				
Pupil does not do well in written assignments, tests and exams.				
Pupil has problems in getting ideas down on paper.				
Pupil writes sentences that are brief, incomplete, disjointed or hard to follow.				
Pupil does not use a wide vocabulary to express ideas.				
Pupil often writes the same words and sentences over and over again.				
Pupil often uses the same format in every type of writing.				
Pupil has difficulties in sequencing sentences in a logical order.				
3. Pupil has spelling difficulties.				59
Pupil makes many spelling errors.				
Pupil makes phonological errors in spelling, such as beg/bec.				
Pupil does not use the correct letters for sounds in words, such as train/tran.				
Pupil makes errors in the use of spelling rules.				
Pupil has repeated spelling errors with common words, such as what/wot.				
Pupil's work is full of spelling corrections made as the pupil writes.				
Pupil successfully learns words for a spelling test but then forgets them.				
4. Pupil has handwriting difficulties.				64
Pupil does not always form letters correctly.				
Pupil's letters and words are often too close together, have irregular spacing or are too widely spaced.				
Pupil prints instead of using cursive writing.				
Pupil's writing begins neatly but quickly becomes messy.				
Pupil takes longer than peers to complete writing tasks, and work is still untidy.				
Pupil's hand gets tired or sweaty after a few minutes of writing.				
5. Pupil finds it difficult to copy accurately.				65

Success with Inclusion © Glynis Hannell, Routledge 2008

Form 2   Written language observation chart *continued*

	Does not apply	Some-times applies	Usually applies	See page
Pupil makes errors when copying words.				
Pupil needs additional time to complete copying in comparison to peers.				
6. Pupil has difficulties with punctuation.				66
Pupil makes errors in punctuation when writing spontaneously.				
Pupil makes more errors than peers when doing formal punctuation.				
7. Pupil has difficulties with proofreading and editing.				67
Pupil overlooks errors when proofreading.				
Teachers often comment, 'Check your work carefully'.				
Pupil may alter correct words during proofreading activities.				
Pupil may replace one error with another one during proofreading.				
Pupil is not able to describe or demonstrate strategies for proofreading.				
Pupil's editing of drafts leaves a significant number of unresolved problems.				
Pupil is not able to describe or evaluate personal writing strategies.				
Pupil does not seek editorial advice or assistance.				
8. Pupil has advanced writing skills.				69
Pupil sometimes produces work of exceptional quality.				
Pupil expresses a love of writing and will write by choice at home or school.				
Pupil has accurate and advanced spelling skills.				
Pupil uses a wide range of vocabulary and expression.				
Pupil uses punctuation accurately and to good effect.				
Pupil can vary writing style to meet various requirements.				
Pupil shows exceptional imagination and creativity in writing.				

Form 3 Mathematics observation chart

	Does not apply	Some-times applies	usually applies	see page
1. Pupil feels negative about mathematics.				72
Pupil expresses dislike of mathematics.				
Pupil lacks confidence in own ability to solve mathematics problems.				
Pupil does not think mathematically in everyday situations.				
Pupil expresses difficulty with mathematics.				
Pupil's mathematics difficulties impact the pupil's classroom achievement.				
Pupil needs additional time to complete mathematics tasks compared to peers.				
2. Pupil has difficulties in understanding the number system.				81
Pupil makes errors when counting.				
Pupil makes errors when working with place value.				
Pupil makes errors in addition and subtraction.				
Pupil does not understand the relationship between addition and subtraction (e.g., cannot use the missing addend to solve subtraction).				
3. Pupil has difficulties with the four operations.				86
Pupil uses tangible objects to count without real understanding.				
Pupil has difficulty applying standard algorithms.				
Pupil makes errors in addition.				
Pupil makes errors in subtraction.				
Pupil makes errors in multiplication.				
Pupil makes errors in division.				
4. Pupil has difficulties with recall.				96
Pupil relies on calculator for basic number facts every time they are needed.				
Pupil makes errors when saying multiplication tables.				
Pupil forgets algorithms.				
Pupil does not solve mathematics problems mentally.				
5. Pupil has difficulties with mathematics problems.				97
Pupil can solve basic mathematics facts but makes errors when choosing which operation to use in a word problem.				
Pupil gets confused about what method to use to solve a word problem.				
6. Pupil has difficulties with spatial reasoning.				97
Pupil does not use concrete mathematics materials effectively.				
Pupil's written numbers and symbols are untidy.				
Pupil's mathematics work is disorganised and difficult to follow.				

Form 3 Mathematics observation chart *continued*

	Does not apply	Some-times applies	usually applies	see page
Pupil expresses confusion when working with spatial mathematics skills.				
7. Pupil has advanced skills in mathematics.				98
Pupil demonstrates advanced mathematical thinking.				
Pupil finds standard class work too easy. Can handle more difficult work.				
Pupil expresses an interest in mathematics and seeks out interesting mathematics challenges.				
Pupil makes negative statements about class mathematics.				

Form 4 Concentration and organisation observation chart

	Does not apply	Some-times applies	Usually applies	See page
1. Pupil is physically restless.				102
Pupil is often active and has a very high energy level.				
Pupil fidgets and moves around even when asked to be still.				
Pupil often touches and fiddles with things.				
Pupil is often loud and hard to quiet down.				
2. Pupil is impulsive and impatient.				105
Pupil acts before thinking.				
Pupil calls out in class.				
Pupil 'forgets' rules and continues to do the wrong thing.				
Pupil rushes through school work and makes silly mistakes.				
Pupil interrupts when others are speaking.				
Pupil pushes in or becomes frustrated when having to wait for turn.				
Pupil gets restless and frustrated when having to wait.				
Pupil often seems to be in a rush.				
Pupil complains if a task or game seems to take too long.				
3. Pupil finds it hard to concentrate.				107
Pupil often looks around and fidgets when supposed to be listening.				
Pupil loses concentration when working on a task.				
Pupil does not see things through to the finish and frequently does not complete the task.				
Pupil starts one thing and gets sidetracked with something else.				
Pupil pays attention to distractions instead of concentrating on task.				
Pupil is inattentive and seems to be in a dream.				
Pupil sometimes does not appear to have heard what is said.				
Pupil does not respond to time pressures.				
Pupil seems vague and unaware of what is going on in the classroom.				
Pupil does not follow instructions.				
Pupil starts something but then drifts off task.				
4. Pupil is poorly organised.				110
Pupil is often unprepared because pupil has not planned ahead.				
Pupil leaves things until the last minute.				
Pupil loses things such as school work, materials or clothing.				
Pupil forgets to bring materials and books when they are needed.				
Pupil is messy, does not keep papers, materials and supplies in order.				
Pupil misses deadlines for handing in work.				

Success with Inclusion © Glynis Hannell, Routledge 2008

Form 5 100 Most frequently used words checklist

	Set 1	✓		Set 2	✓		Set 3	✓		Set 4	✓
1	the		26	or		51	will		76	number	
2	of		27	one		52	up		77	no	
3	and		28	had		53	other		78	way	
4	a		29	by		54	about		79	could	
5	to		30	word		55	out		80	people	
6	in		31	but		56	many		81	my	
7	is		32	not		57	then		82	than	
8	you		33	what		58	them		83	first	
9	that		34	all		59	these		84	water	
10	it		35	were		60	so		85	been	
11	he		36	we		61	some		86	call	
12	was		37	when		62	her		87	who	
13	for		38	your		63	would		88	over	
14	on		39	can		64	make		89	its	
15	are		40	said		65	like		90	now	
16	as		41	there		66	him		91	find	
17	with		42	use		67	into		92	long	
18	his		43	an		68	time		93	down	
19	she		44	each		69	has		94	day	
20	I		45	which		70	look		95	did	
21	at		46	they		71	two		96	get	
22	be		47	do		72	more		97	come	
23	this		48	how		73	write		98	made	
24	have		49	their		74	go		99	may	
25	from		50	if		75	see		100	part	

Form 6 Diagnostic phonics assessment: nonsense word reading

Purpose: This assessment provides a representative sample of the phonic patterns that pupils will encounter as they develop reading skills. Pupils are assessed on their knowledge of letter sounds and their ability to blend sounds together.

Administration: Ask the pupil to 'sound out' each word and then say the whole word. It is important that you hear the pupil do both parts of the task (sounding the word out AND saying the whole word) to make sure that pupils are not guessing at words by sight.

Sample words	Sounds	Whole word	Teacher's notes: Introduction
			Say to the pupil, 'Look, here are some nonsense words. They don't mean anything, but we can still read them. I am going to say the sounds of the letters, and then I am going to say the word. Listen!' Point to each letter as you sound it out, and then say the word.
tob			t-o-b, tob
guk			g-u-k, guk
fab			Say to the pupil, 'You try this one. Say the sounds, and then say the word.' Coach the pupil until the pupil gets it right. Then continue with the rest of the assessment. ✓ if the pupil gives the correct sound for each letter in the nonsense word. ✓ if the pupil says the whole word correctly.
STAGE I	✓	✓	**Three-letter words: Consonant–vowel–consonant** The nonsense words in this section include every letter of the alphabet.
			Teachers: Use this column to make notes and record observations
bam			
dep			
fiv			
jox			
kuz			
gik			
han			
lub			
med			
nif			
pog			
ruk			
quat			
sen			
tib			
von			
wug			
yad			
zed			

Form 6 Diagnostic phonics assessment: nonsense word reading *continued*

STAGE 2	Sounds	Whole word	Two consonants slide together Two consonants make a new sound Final e
steb			
snop			
frade			
crast			
flug			
chite			
brin			
prab			
blat			
yend			
plete			
chim			
shab			
thop			
STAGE 3	Sounds	Whole word	Two vowels make a new sound Vowel and consonant make a new sound Silent letters
neek			
tain			
harb			
maub			
soun			
mawkay			
hoak			
poin			
weam			
rirt			
noomer			
terb			
kneat			
gnorb			
STAGE 4	Sounds	Whole word	Three consonants slide together Four letters make a new sound Words end in 'y' or 'ing'
shrit			
ging			
scrab			
pight			
abtion			
strunning			
hatty			
STAGE 5	Sounds	Whole word	Two patterns combine Compound words with prefixes and suffixes
fadyen			
boinhard			
scribby			
unkeamed			
preteeking			
connotion			

Success with Inclusion © Glynis Hannell, Routledge 2008

Form 7 **Spelling log**

Target word											
Daily practice until five consecutive ✓s are obtained	Date	Date	Date	Date	Date	Date	Date	Date	Date	Date	Date
✓ if correct, ✗ if incorrect											
Weekly practice until four consecutive ✓s are obtained	Date	Date	Date	Date	Date	Date	Date	Date	Date	Date	Date
✓ if correct, ✗ if incorrect											
Monthly practice until three consecutive ✓s are obtained	Date	Date	Date	Date	Date	Date	Date	Date	Date	Date	Date
✓ if correct, ✗ if incorrect											

Target word											
Daily practice until five consecutive ✓s are obtained	Date	Date	Date	Date	Date	Date	Date	Date	Date	Date	Date
✓ if correct, ✗ if incorrect											
Weekly practice until four consecutive ✓s are obtained	Date	Date	Date	Date	Date	Date	Date	Date	Date	Date	Date
✓ if correct, ✗ if incorrect											
Monthly practice until three consecutive ✓s are obtained	Date	Date	Date	Date	Date	Date	Date	Date	Date	Date	Date
✓ if correct, ✗ if incorrect											

Success with Inclusion © Glynis Hannell, Routledge 2008

Form 8 100 minutes reading chart

To be a good reader you have to practice! This chart will help you to see just how much time you spend reading.

Maybe your parent or teacher will agree to give you a small prize or reward if you read for 100 minutes.

Here's what to do. The chart below has 100 squares, one for every minute that you read.

If you read for 4 minutes, colour in 4 squares. If you read for 10 minutes, colour in 10 squares. You can make patterns and use whatever colours you like.

Every time you read colour in more squares – and very soon you will see that you have done 100 minutes of reading.

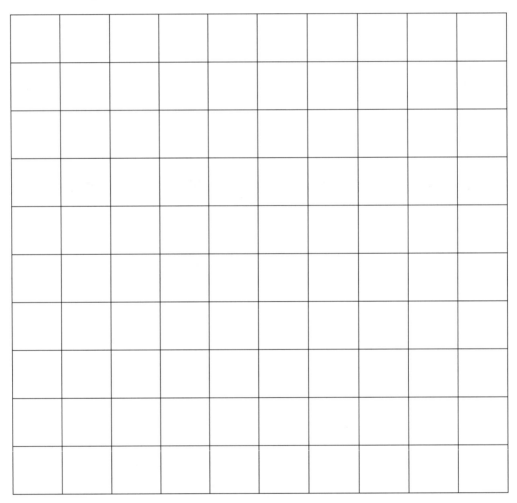

Is every square coloured in? Fantastic! You have read for 100 minutes!

Form 9 New ideas for writing

You can turn real facts into new ideas!

Try this!	Real fact	New idea
Exaggerate Make it extreme		
Substitute Change the detail		
Reverse Switch things around		
Elaborate Make it fancy		
Hypothesise Guess		
Try this!	Real fact	New idea
Exaggerate Make it extreme		
Substitute Change the detail		
Reverse Switch things around		
Elaborate Make it fancy		
Hypothesise Guess		
Try this!	Real fact	New idea
Exaggerate Make it extreme		
Substitute Change the detail		
Reverse Switch things around		
Elaborate Make it fancy		
Hypothesise Guess		
Try this!	Real fact	New idea
Exaggerate Make it extreme		
Substitute Change the detail		
Reverse Switch things around		
Elaborate Make it fancy		

Success with Inclusion © Glynis Hannell, Routledge 2008

Form 10 Punctuation checker

Before you finish your work check your punctuation using this checklist.

Things to look for:	Checked
Correct punctuation at the end of sentences.	
Sentences begin with a capital letter.	
Proper nouns begin with a capital letter.	
Question marks are used where needed.	
Quotation marks are used where needed.	
Commas are used correctly.	
Paragraphs are used correctly.	
Personal watch list. *Write down any punctuation that you forget to use correctly.* *Take **extra** care to look for these every time you check your work.*	

Use this chart and create your own!

Things to look for:	Checked

Form 11 **Counting chart**

Name: _____

1	o											
2	o	o										
3	o	o	o									
4	o	o	o	o								
5	o	o	o	o	o							
6	o	o	o	o	o	o						
7	o	o	o	o	o	o	o					
8	o	o	o	o	o	o	o	o				
9	o	o	o	o	o	o	o	o	o			
10	o	o	o	o	o	o	o	o	o	o		
11	o	o	o	o	o	o	o	o	o	o	o	
12	o	o	o	o	o	o	o	o	o	o	o	o

Form 12 Addition chart

1	1+0									
2	1+1	2+0								
3	1+2	2+1	3+0							
4	1+3	2+2	3+1	4+0						
5	1+4	2+3	3+2	4+1	5+0					
6	1+5	2+4	3+3	4+2	5+1	6+0				
7	1+6	2+5	3+4	4+3	5+2	6+1	7+0			
8	1+7	2+6	3+5	4+4	5+3	6+2	7+1	8+0		
9	1+8	2+7	3+6	4+5	5+4	6+3	7+2	8+1	9+0	
10	1+9	2+8	3+7	4+6	5+5	6+4	7+3	8+2	9+1	10+0

Form 13 Subtraction chart

10	10–0									
9	10–1	9–0								
8	10–2	9–1	8–0							
7	10–3	9–2	8–1	7–0						
6	10–4	9–3	8–2	7–1	6–0					
5	10–5	9–4	8–3	7–2	6–1	5–0				
4	10–6	9–5	8–4	7–3	6–2	5–1	4–0			
3	10–7	9–6	8–5	7–4	6–3	5–2	4–1	3–0		
2	10–8	9–7	8–6	7–5	6–4	5–3	4–2	3–1	2–0	

Form 14 Multiplication chart

	1	2	3	4	5	6	7	8	9	10
1	1	2	3	4	5	6	7	8	9	10
2	2	4	6	8	10	12	14	16	18	20
3	3	6	9	12	15	18	21	24	27	30
4	4	8	12	16	20	24	28	32	36	40
5	5	10	15	20	25	30	35	40	45	50
6	6	12	18	24	30	36	42	48	54	60
7	7	14	21	28	35	42	49	56	63	70
8	8	16	24	32	40	48	56	64	72	80
9	9	18	27	36	45	54	63	72	81	90

Form 15 **Mathematics checklist: addition (single-digit numbers)**

Pupil's name:_____

Date:_____

Use this chart to observe and record the pupil's method of solving the problem.

Provide the pupil with a pencil, paper and counters or blocks. Ask the pupil to complete the addition problem, and observe the working method.

Addition: 4 + 5

Strategy	Pupil response	✓
Uses counters or blocks	Pupil uses blocks or counters.	
Uses fingers	Pupil uses fingers.	
Draws lines or dots to count	Pupil draws and counts lines or dots.	
Does not use support	Pupil says the answer without counting.	
Counts each, counts all	1, 2, 3, 4 1, 2, 3, 4, 5 1, 2, 3, 4, 5, 6, 7, 8, 9	
Counts whole group once	1, 2, 3, 4, 5, 6, 7, 8, 9	
Counts on from first number	5, 6, 7, 8, 9	
Counts on from largest number	6, 7, 8, 9	
Works from a known fact	4 + 4 = 8, 8 + 1 = 9	
Retrieves known fact	9	

Notes on pupil's addition strategies:

Success with Inclusion © Glynis Hannell, Routledge 2008

Form 16 Mathematics checklist: subtraction (single-digit numbers)

Pupil's name: _____

Date: _____

Use this chart to observe and record the pupil's method of solving the problem.

Provide the pupil with a pencil, paper and counters or blocks. Ask the pupil to complete the subtraction problem, and observe the working method.

Subtraction: 8 – 3

Strategy	Pupil response	✓
Uses counters or blocks	Pupil uses blocks or counters.	
Uses fingers	Pupil uses fingers.	
Draws lines or dots to count	Pupil draws and counts lines or dots.	
Does not use support	Pupil says the answer without counting.	
Counts all and then counts back	1, 2, 3, 4, 5, 6, 7, 8, 7, 6, 5	
Counts back from largest number	7, 6, 5	
Counts up from lowest number	4, 5, 6, 7, 8	
Works from a known fact	8 – 2 = 6, 6 – 1 = 5	
Retrieves known fact	5	

Notes on pupil's subtraction strategies:

Success with Inclusion © Glynis Hannell, Routledge 2008

Form 17 Mathematics checklist: multiplication

Pupil's name: _____

Date: _____

Use this chart to observe and record the pupil's method of solving the problem.

Provide the pupil with a pencil, paper and counters or blocks. Ask the pupil to complete the multiplication problem, and observe the working method.

Multiplication: 4 × 5

Strategy	Pupil response	✓
Uses counters or blocks	Pupil uses blocks or counters.	
Uses fingers	Pupil uses fingers.	
Draws diagram of scattered lines or dots	Pupil draws and counts lines or dots.	
Draws diagram of orderly lines or dots	Pupil draws and counts lines or dots.	
Does not use support	Pupil says the answer without counting.	
Counts up in fives	5, 10, 15, 20	
Counts up in fours	4, 8, 12, 16, 20	
Recites times table	$1 \times 5 = 5$, $2 \times 5 = 10$, $3 \times 5 = 15$, $4 \times 5 = 20$	
Works from a known fact	$5 \times 5 = 25$, $25 - 5 = 20$	
Retrieves known fact	20	

Notes on pupil's multiplication strategies:

Form 18 **Mathematics checklist: division**

Pupil's name: _____

Date: _____

Use this chart to observe and record the pupil's method of solving the problem.

Provide the pupil with a pencil, paper and counters or blocks. Ask the pupil to complete the division problem, and observe the working method.

Division: 15 ÷ 3

Strategy	Pupil response	✓
Uses counters or blocks	Pupil uses blocks or counters.	
Uses fingers	Pupil uses fingers.	
Draws diagram of scattered lines or dots	Pupil draws and counts lines or dots.	
Draws diagram of orderly lines or dots	Pupil draws and counts lines or dots.	
Does not use support	Pupil says the answer without counting.	
Counts off groups of 3	1, 2, 3, 1, 2, 3 1, 2, 3 1, 2, 3 1, 2, 3	
Counts in threes	3, 6, 9, 12, 15 *or* 15, 12, 9, 6, 3	
Works from a known fact	5 + 5 + 5 = 15	
Retrieves known fact	5	

Notes on pupil's division strategies:

Form 19 **Mathematics checklist: addition (two two-digit numbers, no regrouping)**

Pupil's name: _____

Date: _____

Use this chart to observe and record the pupil's method of solving the problem.

Provide the pupil with a pencil, paper and counters or blocks. Ask the pupil to complete the addition problem, and observe the working method.

Two-digit addition: 14
                          +25

Strategy	Pupil response	✓
Deals with 14 and 25 as whole numbers	14+25=	
Counts from 14	15, 16, 17, …	
Counts from 25	26, 27, 28, …	
Works with columns	4+5= 1+2=	
Starts to work on right-hand column first	Works on 4+5=, then 1+2=	
Adds columns by counting	Counts to obtain total for each column	
Starts to work on right-hand side of sum		
Adds coumns, uses known facts	Writes in answer without counting	

Notes on pupil's addition strategies:

Form 20 **Mathematics checklist: addition
(two two-digit numbers, with regrouping)**

Pupil's name: _____

Date: _____

Use this chart to observe and record the pupil's method of solving the problem.

Provide the pupil with a pencil, paper and counters or blocks. Ask the pupil to complete the addition problem, and observe the working method.

Two-digit addition: 27
                          +35

Checkpoints	Observations
Is the pupil using the method taught in your class correctly?	
Is the pupil using counting to calculate the answers for each column?	
How does the pupil handle the regrouping of 7+5=12?	
How does the pupil handle the 10s column?	
Notes on pupil's addition strategies:	

Success with Inclusion © Glynis Hannell, Routledge 2008

Form 21 **Mathematics checklist: subtraction
(two two-digit numbers, no exchanging)**

Pupil's name: _____

Date: _____

Use this chart to observe and record the pupil's method of solving the problem.

Provide the pupil with a pencil, paper and counters or blocks. Ask the pupil to complete the subtraction problem, and observe the working method.

Two-digit subtraction: 28
   −13

Strategy	Pupil response	✓
Deals with 28 and 13 as whole numbers	28−13=	
Counts down from 28	27, 26, 25, …	
Counts up from 13	14, 15, 16, …	
Works with columns	8−3= 2−1=	
Subtracts columns by counting	Counts to obtain total for each column	
Starts to work on right-hand side first	Works on 8−3=, then 2−1=	
Subtracts using known facts	Writes in answer without calculating	

Notes on pupil's subtraction strategies:

Success with Inclusion © Glynis Hannell, Routledge 2008

Form 22 Mathematics checklist: subtraction (two two-digit numbers, with exchanging)

Pupil's name: _____

Date: _____

Use this chart to observe and record the pupil's method of solving the problem.

Provide the pupil with a pencil, paper and counters or blocks. Ask the pupil to complete the subtraction problem, and observe the working method.

Two-digit subtraction: 32
                             −15

Checkpoints	Observations
Is the pupil using the method taught in your class correctly?	
Is the pupil using counting to calculate the answers for each column?	
How does the pupil handle the exchanging required for 2–5?	
How does the pupil handle the 10s column?	
Notes on pupil's subtraction strategies:	

Form 23 Teacher checklist for mastery learning

Pupil's name: _____

Date: _____

Write a clear description of the task:

	Monday	Tuesday	Wednesday	Thursday	Friday	Saturday	Sunday
✓							
✓							
✓							
✓							
✓							
✓							
✓							
✓							

Has the pupil succeeded on three consecutive days?	YES: Wait one week and check again. The next check will be on _____[date]. NO: If the pupil cannot achieve three successes after a reasonable period of instruction and practice, then the task is too difficult and should be revised.
Is the pupil able to succeed one week later?	YES: Wait four weeks and check again. The next check will be on _____[date]. NO: Go back and practice some more until the pupil gets another three successes in a row, then try the one-week wait again.
Is the pupil able to succeed four weeks later?	YES: Congratulations!! The pupil has mastered the task. NO: Go back and practice some more until the pupil gets another three successes in a row, then try the one-week wait again.

Success with Inclusion © Glynis Hannell, Routledge 2008

Form 24 Teacher checklist for successful learning

For the pupil to have the best chance of successful learning, all the items should be checked Yes.

	Yes	Not sure	No
The pupil understands the purpose of the learning.			
The pupil knows the learning goal(s).			
The pupil expectations are realistic.			
The pupil understands how the current lesson connects to previous learning.			
The pupil is confident that they will be able to learn what is being taught.			
The pupil is not criticised, punished or ridiculed if a mistake is made.			
The learning is at the correct level of difficulty. It is not too hard or too easy for the pupil.			
Complex tasks are broken down into small sequential steps.			
Teaching is explicit.			
Teaching is carefully structured.			
The teacher has shown the pupil what to do.			
The teacher asks questions to guide learning.			
The pupil can see their own progress.			
The pupil is encouraged to evaluate their own learning.			
The pupil is provided with guided practice. The teacher monitors and guides the pupil toward success.			
The pupil continues to practice until the pupil is 100 per cent sure of what to do.			
Mistakes are used as information. The pupil and teacher look at mistakes to understand what went wrong.			
The pupil is encouraged to think aloud, so the teacher can understand the pupil's learning process.			
Observations and notes			

Form 25 Teacher: personal profile as an inclusive teacher

This personal checklist will help you determine areas in which you feel you are doing well and areas where you may want to make some positive changes.

	No	Some-times or maybe	Yes
Organising an inclusive classroom			
I always make detailed plans for my daily teaching.			
My daily teaching plan includes accommodations and modifications for pupils with special needs.			
I keep careful records of intervention and inclusive strategies that have been used in my class.			
I keep accurate, up-to-date records of each pupil's progress.			
Teaching in an inclusive classroom			
I deal with most pupil behaviour problems successfully.			
I am flexible and use a range of teaching strategies to support pupils who have learning difficulties.			
I have developed a good collection of resources to help me meet the needs of all my pupils.			
Most pupils make good personal progress in my class.			
I willingly accommodate pupils with difficulties in my class by modifying and adapting the curriculum and the assignments.			
I have a positive and inclusive attitude towards all pupils in my class, regardless of their learning or behavioural difficulties.			
I enjoy teaching pupils of all abilities.			
I am patient and supportive when pupils find learning difficult.			
I am patient and supportive when pupils have emotional or behavioural problems.			
When my pupils with special needs become adults, I think they will look back and remember my class positively.			
Working with colleagues and parents			
My colleagues and I support each other in assisting pupils with learning difficulties and disabilities.			
I am prepared to seek help from colleagues.			
I know whom to ask when I need additional support or materials to support a pupil with special needs.			
When I meet with parents, our discussions are usually constructive and positive.			
I understand when parents are upset, angry or worried about their pupil's difficulties and can offer positive, practical solutions.			
I meet frequently with my colleagues to discuss how our pupils are doing and what further support is needed.			
I think parents of pupils with special needs feel that I respect their views and that I am doing my best for their child.			
Professional development for inclusive teaching			
My school offers enough training and support opportunities for developing inclusive teaching skills.			
I keep up to date with new ideas in inclusive teaching.			

Success with Inclusion © Glynis Hannell, Routledge 2008

Form 26 Teacher chart for planning an inclusive programme

Pupil's name: _____

Date: _____

General Education Teacher: _____

Special Education Teacher: _____

Other Team Members: _____

Barriers to successful inclusion and learning	Specific strategies to be implemented	Person responsible	Resources needed
Pupil has physical or sensory special needs.			
Pupil has trouble understanding basic classroom instructions and/or assignments.			
When a topic is taught to the class, the pupil often has trouble grasping the ideas.			
Pupil has difficulties reading worksheets and curriculum materials.			
Pupil reads very slowly. A lot of class time is taken up with reading class work, assignments or tests.			
Pupil has difficulties in understanding what has been read.			
Pupil has difficulties expressing in writing.			
Pupil has difficulties with locating the key information when researching a topic.			

Barriers to successful inclusion and learning	Specific strategies to be implemented	Person responsible	Resources needed
Pupil has difficulties organising information and ideas into a logical sequence.			
Pupil has difficulties with spelling and punctuation.			
Pupil has difficulties copying things down quickly and accurately.			
Pupil's understanding of mathematics concepts and methods is below the expected level for the pupil's age.			
Pupil is slow and inaccurate with mental mathematics.			
Pupil does not participate in class activities and discussion or ask for help when it is needed.			
Pupil has difficulties concentrating on what is being taught.			
Pupil does not finish the tasks and assignments in the allotted time period.			
Pupil's poor organisational skills are a barrier to successful learning.			
Pupil is anxious, frustrated or negative towards learning because of difficulties.			
Behavioural, social or emotional problems (not related to learning difficulties) interfere with pupil's progress.			

Form 27 Teacher guide to writing pupil goals

Pupil's name: _____

Date: _____

AREA OF CONCERN Note area of concern.	
ACHIEVEMENTS What can the pupil already achieve in this area?	
GOAL What is the goal set for the pupil?	
METHOD How are you going to work towards this goal?	
TIMEFRAME When do you expect to reach this goal?	
ASSESSMENT How will you assess whether or not the pupil has reached the goal?	

Success with Inclusion © Glynis Hannell, Routledge 2008

Form 28 Teacher notes: getting ready for a meeting

Teacher: _____ Pupil: _____ Date: _____

What positive things you would like to say about the pupil?
What are your main concerns about the pupil?
What strategies seem to work best for the pupil?
Are there any strategies or situations that seem to increase or emphasise the problems?
Why do you think the pupil is having these difficulties?
What plans do you have for intervention or support over the next two months?
What are the school's longer term plans for meeting the pupil's needs?
Is there any information that you want to give the parents?
Are there any questions that you would like to ask the parent[s]?
Are there any questions that you would like to ask your professional colleagues?
What assistance do you need to meet the pupil's needs?
How do you think the pupil views the situation?
What do you hope the meeting will achieve?
Additional areas to address:

Success with Inclusion © Glynis Hannell, Routledge 2008

Form 29 Teacher: meeting record

(Provide copies to everyone attending the meeting.)

Date of the meeting: _____ Pupil's name: _____

People in attendance: _____

_____

_____

Record keeper: _____

What was discussed at the meeting?   Make a note of who spoke and what they said.

List the decisions. Make a note of what was agreed to and who is responsible for the implementation.

Form 30 Pupil guide to making changes

Let's look at the things you are good at and things that maybe you are not so good at. See if there are any changes that would be good to make.

How do you rate yourself with **friendliness**?

Very low   Average   Very high
OOOOOOOOOOOOOOOOOOOOOOOOOOOOOOOOOOOOOOOOOOOOOOO

How could you make your rating go higher?

Write three ways you could improve your personal rating for friendliness.

1. _____

2. _____

3. _____

How do you rate yourself with **reading**?

Very low   Average   Very high
OOOOOOOOOOOOOOOOOOOOOOOOOOOOOOOOOOOOOOOOOOOOOOO

How could you make your rating go higher?

Write three ways you could improve your personal rating for reading.

1. _____

2. _____

3. _____

Success with Inclusion © Glynis Hannell, Routledge 2008

How do you rate yourself with **concentration**?

Very low   Average   Very high

OOOOOOOOOOOOOOOOOOOOOOOOOOOOOOOOOOOOOOOOOOOOOOOOOOO

How could you make your rating go higher?

Write three ways you could improve your personal rating for concentration.

1. _____

2. _____

3. _____

How do you rate yourself with **personal organisation**?

Very low   Average   Very high

OOOOOOOOOOOOOOOOOOOOOOOOOOOOOOOOOOOOOOOOOOOOOOOOOOO

How could you make your rating go higher?

Write three ways you could improve your personal rating for personal organisation.

1. _____

2. _____

3. _____

How do you rate yourself with **spelling and writing**?

Very low   Average   Very high
OOOOOOOOOOOOOOOOOOOOOOOOOOOOOOOOOOOOOOOOOOOOOOOOOO

How could you make your rating go higher?

Write three ways you could improve your personal rating for spelling and writing.

1. _____

2. _____

3. _____

How do you rate yourself with **mathematics**?

Very low   Average   Very high
OOOOOOOOOOOOOOOOOOOOOOOOOOOOOOOOOOOOOOOOOOOOOOOOOO

How could you make your rating go higher?

Write three ways you could improve your personal rating for mathematics.

1. _____

2. _____

3. _____

How do you rate yourself with _____?

Very low   Average   Very high

OOOOOOOOOOOOOOOOOOOOOOOOOOOOOOOOOOOOOOOOOOOOOOOOOOOOO

How could you make your rating go higher?

Write three ways you could improve your personal rating for this subject.

1. _____

2. _____

3. _____

How do you rate yourself with _____?

Very low   Average   Very high

OOOOOOOOOOOOOOOOOOOOOOOOOOOOOOOOOOOOOOOOOOOOOOOOOOOOO

How could you make your rating go higher?

Write three ways you could improve your personal rating for this subject.

1. _____

2. _____

3. _____

Form 31 Pupil work planner

Task to be done:	Date to be completed	✓ Done
Getting started: Things to do to get started For example: Visit the library and get reference books. Make a folder. Highlight key words in question.		
Stages of work to be done: For example: Take notes from all the references. Write an outline. Discuss the outline with the teacher. Write the introduction.		
Wrapping up: Final stages before completion For example: Proofread and edit the final draft. Prepare the cover sheet. Hand in for grading.		

Form 32 Pupil priorities chart

Step 1: Write a list of all the things you have to do today.
Step 2: Number the items on the list in order of importance.
Step 3: Check the items off as you finish them.

Order of importance	What do I have to do today?	Done ✓

Form 33 Pupil guide to setting goals

Note to teachers: Work through this sheet with the pupil to help select and clarify personal goals.

Long-term goals

My dream is that when I am an adult:

I will be working as a _____

I will be living in _____

I will have _____

Medium-term goals

By this time next year I hope that:

I will have improved in _____

I will have succeeded at _____

I will have started to _____

My achievements

You may need to talk to your teacher about what to put in this section.

Write down three things you have already achieved. For example: I can already sound out words with single sounds. I can already read all the Level 1 books. I can already add two single numbers together.

I can already _____

I can already _____

I can already _____

My short-term goals for the next four weeks

Ask your teacher to help you with this.

Talk to your teacher and choose some goals that you think you can achieve. For example: In the next four weeks, I am aiming to read three Level 2 books. In the next four weeks, my goal is to learn how to sound out words with ch, sh and ee in them. In the next four weeks, I will try to learn how to add two double-digit numbers together.

Goal 1 In the next four weeks, I am aiming to _____

Goal 2 In the next four weeks I am aiming to _____

Goal 3 In the next four weeks I am aiming to _____

If I achieve these goals my reward(s) will be:

Goal 1 _____

Goal 2 _____

Goal 3 _____

Success with Inclusion © Glynis Hannell, Routledge 2008

Form 34 **Pupil plan for getting organised**

Use this chart to keep a record of what went wrong with your organisation. Maybe you forgot to take the correct book to class, or perhaps you did not allow yourself enough time between classes.

Write down the excuse or reason you messed up. Then write down a solution for next time.

Date	My excuse. What went wrong?	How can I fix it next time?

Form 35 **Pupil self-evaluation**

How hard did I try?

☐ I tried pretty hard.

☐ I was OK.

☐ I could have tried harder.

How did the work turn out?

☐ I am pleased with what I did.

☐ I think that what I did is OK.

☐ I am disappointed with the work.

What are the best things about this piece of work?

_____

_____

_____

What would I like to change?

_____

_____

_____

How does this work compare?

☐ It is better than anything I have done before.

☐ It is about the same as my other work.

☐ It is not as good as some my other work.

What will my teacher think?

☐ My teacher will be really pleased.

☐ My teacher will think it is OK.

☐ My teacher will say I could have done better.

Form 36 Pupil: what I think about school

Name: _____

	No	Sometimes Maybe	Yes
I enjoy coming to school.			
I like the way my teacher teaches me.			
The other pupils in my class are friendly.			
The work in my class is easy for me.			
I feel worried about my school work.			
Reading is difficult for me.			
Spelling and writing are difficult for me.			
Mathematics is difficult for me.			
My teacher helps me if I do not understand.			
I like reading.			
I like spelling and writing.			
I like mathematics.			
Other pupils hassle or bully me.			
I am well organised.			
It is OK to ask the teacher if you need help.			
I concentrate well in school.			
I try my best in school.			
The other pupils are smarter than I am.			
My family is proud of how I do in school.			
I wish the teachers gave us easier work.			
I wish the teachers gave us harder work.			
We have fun in our class.			
We do interesting things in our class.			
I get in trouble when it is not my fault.			
Other pupils think I am smart.			
I worry about getting into trouble at school.			
I follow the rules in school.			
The other pupils in school are kind to me.			
The teacher is fair to everyone in our class.			
I think I need more help with my school work.			
I think I will get a good school report this year.			

Three wishes for school:
I wish that . . .

1. _____

2. _____

3. _____

Form 37 Pupil reward cards

Photocopy this page, and use the cards to recognise and reward pupils' efforts with concentration, organisation and perseverance. The blank cards can be used to write your own messages. You can offer a small prize once a pupil has collected a number of these cards. Write the pupil's name on each card to personalise it.

The cards may be decorated with glitter, stickers and sequins to make them look very special!

You stayed on task until you finished today. *Well done!* *Awarded to*	*You ignored the distractions very well.* *Fantastic job!* *Awarded to* ....
I noticed you listened very well today. *Great work!* *Awarded to*	*You remembered to bring everything you needed today.* *Congratulations!* *Awarded to* ....
That was a tough task, but you did it. *Well done!* *Awarded to*	*You are so well organised.* *You are a great example to others!* *Awarded to* ....
You did not stop once. *You just kept working.* *I love it!* *Awarded to*	*You waited your turn so well today.* *That's terrific!* *Awarded to* ....
    Awarded to	 *Awarded to* ....

Form 38 Pupil guide to 'I can do'

Note to teachers: Look over this sheet, and work through both sections with the pupil. Use the items as discussion points to help the pupil develop a CAN DO attitude.

What you say to yourself makes a BIG difference to whether or not you succeed.

Check out these statements and decide if you think they will help you succeed—or not.

You are out on the sports field for a training session with the coach. This is what you say to yourself:	Yes! This will help me to succeed!	No! This will not help me succeed.
This is too hard! I can't do it. I give up!		
Practice is boring, but it's got to be done.		
This is too hard to learn. I'm not doing it.		
This is hard to learn. I'll ask the coach for some help.		
I've tried this move three times already. Maybe I need to do it five or six times before I get it right.		
I don't like practising. It's boring, and I'm not doing it.		
I am not giving up. I will keep going until I succeed.		
I won't be able to do that. No way.		
That looks hard, but I can give it a try.		
Just do it!		
I can't!		

Like everyone in your class, you will find some learning difficult and some learning easy. Having a CAN DO attitude will make it easier for you to handle the difficult work successfully.

Look at each of these, and decide whether A or B is the CAN DO attitude.

You have tried the mathematics problem twice, and you still cannot figure it out.
A. You give up and put your mathematics book away.
B. You give it one more try and then ask the teacher for help.

The book you have to read for class is taking a long time to get through.
A. You put in some extra time, and you ask someone to read some of it to you.
B. You put the book away and forget about it.

The assignment your teacher has set looks really difficult.
A.   You get started and give it a try. You check in with your teacher for help if needed.
B.   You don't get started, because it looks too hard.

The teacher has asked for volunteers to help but has not told you what you will have to do.
A. You think it might be difficult or boring, so you do not put your hand up.
B. You think it might be interesting. At least it is worth finding out. You put your hand up.

CAN DO!

Here are some CAN DO statements that you can copy, cut out and put where you see them often. How about on your book covers, your wall by your desk, your computer or your school desk?

WHEN THE GOING GETS TOUGH, THE TOUGH GET GOING.

JUST DO IT!

I DON'T GIVE UP, 'CAUSE I'M A HERO!

I never give up and never give in!

IF I CAN DREAM IT, I CAN DO IT.

If at first I don't succeed, I try, try again.

DON'T QUIT: WINNERS NEVER QUIT!

THINK BIG. YOU CAN DO IT!

If I think I can, I can!

Form 39 Pupil notes: getting ready for a meeting

Your name:_____

Date:_____

What are the good things about school right now?

How do you think you are doing at school?

Are you worried about anything at school?

Is anything at school upsetting you or making you angry?

What sorts of things would make school better for you?

What sorts of things would make school worse for you?

Can you think of ways you can deal with any of the problems you are experiencing?

What would you like the teachers to do to help you?

Is there anything you want to tell the teachers?

Are there any questions you would like to ask the teachers?

What sorts of things do you enjoy outside of school?

How can your family help you best?

Who is the person at school you feel you can talk to best if you have a problem?

Soon you will be having a meeting with your teachers and family. What do you hope will happen at the meeting?

Form 40 Parent guide to reading at home

Learning to read is an important skill, and most pupils take several years to master the basics. Reading at home can really help your child develop good reading skills.

- Make reading practice a part of your daily routine. Choose a regular time and place, and whenever possible, stick to this.

- Talk to your child's teacher about your child's progress and how you can help with reading practice at home.

- For younger children, or those older pupils who find reading difficult, practicing early in the day (before school) might be better than after school, when your child is tired.

- If you are free during the day, you may be able to go into school to help your child with extra reading practice.

- Try to make the reading sessions relaxed and pleasant for both you and your child. If your child gets anxious about reading, progress will be slower. Sitting together in a comfortable chair, or even cuddled up on the bed, can be a good place to practice reading where you both feel relaxed.

- Reading time at home can sometimes be a very stressful situation. If upsets seem unavoidable, see if another family member, family friend or tutor can help your child.

- Make sure that the child's reading material is suitable. It needs to be easy enough to read with enjoyment and suitable to your child's interests. Talk to the teacher if you feel that your child has a book that is too easy or too hard, or not interesting.

- Pupils who find reading difficult generally need a highly structured program, where books are read in a sequence of difficulty and where there is a lot of repetition. Talk to the teacher about this if you are unsure.

- Read for a specific period of time. Ten minutes of reading is long enough for a younger pupil. This time can be increased gradually up to about 20 minutes for the older pupil. Knowing that the reading session will end at a definite time helps to encourage the reluctant reader.

- For the very reluctant reader, start with very short, easy reading sessions, and gradually increase the time.

- For the reluctant reader, provide an incentive for reading. For instance, provide a small reward for every 10 minutes of reading, and if necessary, you can add a bonus for good attitude.

- Remember to teach, not to test. When you teach, you help your child to succeed by providing as much help as needed and by praising and encouraging. (When you test, the child does not get any help, and they are judged while reading.)

Success with Inclusion © Glynis Hannell, Routledge 2008

- Make sure that the reading book is easy enough for your child to read with only a little assistance. Make sure that the book is of interest to your child.

- If your child wants to read a book that is much too difficult, read the book aloud, or take turns reading a page, or read along together.

- If your child gets stuck on a word, silently count to four before you help.

- Sound the word out, and say it to your child; e.g., 'm-a-tch, match'. Do not add extra comment, just demonstrate the sounding out and saying the word, and then allow your child to continue.

- If the word cannot be sounded out, just tell your child the word, and allow your child to continue.

- If your child makes a mistake on a word but continues reading and picks up the story, simply continue.

- If your child gets confused, take the child back to where the errors began. Read the section out loud, and then let your child read it again. If necessary, read along with your child until you arrive at an easier part that the child can read without help.

- When your child has finished reading, go back over any words for which you provided help. Have your child practice sounding out the words, and reread the sentence in which the errors occurred.

- Let your child prepare to read before a final 'performance.' Look at the pictures, read the title and discuss what the story might be about. Read the story to your child, and encourage your child to practice reading it. Allow your child to practice until he feels ready to read 'for real.'

- Some children like the idea of a 'performance.' Your child may like to read the story to another adult or record the story for another family member, friend or younger sibling.

- Some children like to use a scoring system, where the progress is measured by reducing errors and increasing speed. You can use a stopwatch or kitchen timer to determine how the speed increases with each practice session.

- Audio cassette tapes can be used for practice. The child can listen to the story on tape until ready to read it alone or can read along with the tape during practice.

- Always encourage reading comprehension by discussing the selections that your child has read, including the pictures and information obtained.

- Having your child ask you questions about the reading is a very good way of developing comprehension. Asking an adult questions takes pressure off the child.

Success with Inclusion © Glynis Hannell, Routledge 2008

Form 41 **Parent guide to mathematics at home**

Parents can play an important part in helping their children develop confidence and good skills in mathematics. But that does not mean you have to give them sheets of sums or drill them with times tables. Mathematics is a real-life subject, so help your children notice and use the mathematics that is all around you at home and in the neighborhood. You will provide your children with a strong basis and a good start for the school mathematics curriculum.

Here are some ideas to help get your children working with numbers and mathematics at home.

- Point out the mathematics around them. How much does that box of cookies weigh? How much does it cost to get into the movies? What is the latest score in the game?

- Involve your children in practical activities that use mathematics. Cook with them and show them how to follow the instructions and measure the ingredients. Does the fence need fixing? Let them help you measure the fence. Take them with you to the hardware store to purchase the materials you need.

- Give children an allowance, and teach them how to budget and save.

- Use sports to teach mathematics. How many runs does the home team need to get ahead? How far from the record was that time?

- Teach them to be serious shoppers. Show them how to compare prices and find a good buy at the store.

- Have them look at the sales receipts from your shopping trip. Which item cost the most? What was the total cost of your shopping? Did you pay more than the price advertised by the store down the road?

- Keep a calendar and a clock at home, and show your children how to use both. Encourage the children to check off on the days on the calendar as they wait for a birthday or special day.

- Show children how to use the TV guide and the clock to catch their favorite programs.

- Have the children take part in planning a family outing. Incorporate as many mathematics skills as possible. How long will the journey take? What time will you leave? Discuss money. How much will it cost to go into the show? What much gas will the car need? What is the price per gallon?

- Play family games for fun in the car. Look at the license plates of the cars around you. Who can find the largest number on a plate? Who is the first to see a number 2, or three numbers that add up to 10? Who can see a license plate that has only odd numbers on it? Who can find a plate that has only even numbers?

- Talk to the teacher about the sort of mathematics your children are doing in school. If you do help with school mathematics assignments, be sure you are using the same method your child is learning in class.

Form 42 **Parent notes: getting ready for a meeting**

Your name: _____ Child's name: _____ Date: _____

What positive things would you like to say about your child?

What are your main concerns about your child?

What seems to work best for your child?

Does anything seem to increase or emphasise your child's problems?

Why do you think your child is having these difficulties?

What do you hope the school will be able to do for your child?

Is there anything you can tell the teachers to help them understand your child better?

Are there any questions you would like to ask the teachers?

Have you found anything outside of school to help your child?

What help do you need from the teachers or other professionals?

How do you think your child views the situation?

What do you hope the meeting will achieve?

Success with Inclusion © Glynis Hannell, Routledge 2008